A CONCISE SURVEY OF AMERICAN LITERATURE

By Alan Wykes:

NOVELS

PURSUIT TILL MORNING
THE MUSIC SLEEPING
THE PEN FRIEND
HAPPYLAND

PLAY

SURRENDER AT NOON

A CONCISE SURVEY OF AMERICAN LITERATURE

by

ALAN WYKES

LIBRARY PUBLISHERS
NEW YORK

First Published in the U.S.A., 1955
by
Library Publishers
8 West 40th Street, New York 18, N.Y.

Printed in Great Britain
for Library Publishers
by
Morrison and Gibb Ltd., London and Edinburgh

TO

R. A. U.

ACKNOWLEDGEMENTS

I WOULD like to thank the undermentioned publishers, agents and individual copyright-owners for their permission to quote from copyright material:

The Macmillan Company, New York, for the poems 'Charles Carville' and 'Cavender's House' by Edward Arlington Robinson.

The Liveright Publishing Corporation, New York, for the poem 'Mid-Day,' by Hilda Doolittle, from *Collected Poems of H. D.*, published by Liveright Publishers, New York, copyright 1954, by Hilda Doolittle.

Harper & Brothers, New York, for the poems 'Yet Do I Marvel,' from *Color*, by Countee Cullen, copyright 1952, by Harper & Brothers, copyright 1953, by Ida M. Cullen; and 'The Love Tree' from *Copper Sun*, by Countee Cullen, copyright 1927, by Harper & Brothers.

The Houghton Mifflin Company, Boston, for the extract from *The Outcasts of Poker Flat*, by Bret Harte.

Random House Inc., New York, for the extract from the poem 'Don Rafael A Nephew,' from *Tender Buttons*, by Gertrude Stein, and the extracts from *Tamar and Other Poems*, by Robinson Jeffers.

Charles Scribner's Sons Ltd., New York, for the extract from *Posson Jane*, by George W. Cable.

Alfred A. Knopf Inc., New York, for the extract from 'A Gold Slipper' from *Youth and the Bright Medusa*, by Willa Cather.

C. D. Medley, Esq., for the extract from *Esther Waters*, by George Moore.

Hughes Massie & Co. Ltd., for the extracts from *A Story Teller's Story* and *Hands*, by Sherwood Anderson.

Pearn, Pollinger & Higham Ltd., and the F. Scott Fitzgerald Estate, for the extract from *The Great Gatsby*, by F. Scott Fitzgerald.

John Lane the Bodley Head Ltd., for the extract from *The Demiurge*, by James Branch Cabell.

Routledge & Kegan Paul Ltd., for the extract from the essay 'How Studs Lonigan was Written,' from *The League of Frightened Philistines*, by James T. Farrell.

Faber & Faber Ltd., for the extracts from *Sweeney Among the Nightingales* and *The Use of Poetry and the Use of Criticism*, by T. S. Eliot, O.M.

William Faulkner and Chatto & Windus Ltd., for the Nobel Prize Address and extracts from *Sartoris*, *Pylon*, *Intruder in the Dust* and *Sanctuary*, by William Faulkner.

And Mrs E. Royall Tyler for the extract from *Ethan Frome*, by Edith Wharton.

My efforts to trace Mrs Theodore Dreiser, beneficial owner of the copyright in the works of Theodore Dreiser, have been unsuccessful and I have therefore been unable to ask her permission to use the extract from *The Financier*.

A. W.

CONTENTS

INTRODUCTION

There are several excellent histories of American literature in existence. For various reasons none of them answers the demands of the particular audience for whom I intend this concise survey. Some of them are obtainable with varying degrees of readiness from the libraries by those who care to ferret for them; others have been forced into oblivion by war, wear and tear and sundry of the hazards of publishing; most of them are either too exhaustive or too outdated for the needs of the readers I have in mind.

The audience for this book exists, I believe, in the growing number who are beginning to find themselves involved in American literature not because of any academic desire but because historic and scientific happenings have involved them. *No Man is an Iland:* least of all is he an island when a foreign literature is in a language similar to his own and the ocean dividing him from the work of writers in which he fondly thinks he has little concern can be crossed physically in half a day—both ways.

This is not a work of criticism—anyway, not designedly: the academic student seeking the answers to searching questions on American literature will find little of more than introductory value to him here, and much of that will be in the bibliography—which I have made as complete as possible within the bounds of expedience. Nor is it, I hope, a mere catalogue of names. I have tried to make it precisely what the title says it is.

With the bestowal of the Nobel prize for literature for 1949 on William Faulkner and the bestowal of the same award on Ernest Hemingway in 1954, American literature has now achieved a glamorous as well as an aesthetic value. The works of these and other American writers are filmed for mass communication and at the same time spoken of in hushed voices by literary coteries—the degree of hush usually increasing in inverse ratio to the critical awareness of the coterie concerned; so that the ordinary reader who has given up his half-hearted struggle for insularity and merely wants to discover what all the fuss is about and what Messrs Faulkner and Hemingway and the others have to say about life and people is a little puzzled. He is puzzled because he is less aware of the circumstances that have gone to the making of American literature than he is of the circumstances that have created the literary climate of, say, France. It is for this reader—more or less specifically—that I have planned this book.

A. W.

CHAPTER ONE

Early Literature

I

THE literature of any nation cannot be said to have established itself until it has produced something unique. Literature thrives on the premise that men cherish their national, regional and parochial associations. The idea of a common literature of the whole world is as horrid as the idea of a common language. The monumental dullness of Esperanto would be exceeded ten thousand times by the utter dreariness of Unilit if such a conception ever became feasible—which heaven forfend.

But a unique national literature cannot be summoned from nothing: it is the product of that nation's happiness and suffering, of the racial characteristics of the people, and of the influences of other and earlier literatures.

There is no arbitrary relationship between the time in which a nation may be said to have established itself and the time the uniqueness of its literature takes to emerge—nor indeed any certainty that such a quality of uniqueness ever will emerge. (English literature *per se* began in the fourteenth century; Syrian literature *per se* hasn't begun yet, though the Syrian nation is somewhat older than the English. There is of course a Syrian literature, but it has marked time since the first dynasty of Babylon, never having shaken itself free from the Akkadian and Sumerian literatures from which it sprang. And historic events have now overcome the necessity for it to do so.) But there is of necessity every relationship between the literature of a nation and the literatures from which it derives until its unique quality does emerge. Sometimes the relationship continues in varying degrees beyond the time of such emergence—particularly when the languages concerned are similar, as in the literatures of England and America.

In considering English literature it is convenient for historic reasons to begin with Chaucer; but it happens to be a fact that Chaucer was the first uniquely English writer—the six centuries of English literature that preceded him were formative and influential only. In considering American literature it is convenient to begin with Washington Irving; but it happens not to be true that Irving was the first uniquely American writer. He is one of the writers occupying a position in American literature similar to the position in English literature of the pre-Chaucerian writers of chronicles and narrative poems—except that what he has to say is comprehensible without translation. But before him, and after him, were other writers and other influences that have to be considered before we get to Whitman, who was the first poet to make literature speak for America as Chaucer made it speak for England. And although it may be mildly boring to attend to a recital of the traditions and influences that were forming American literature two hundred years before Irving was born it is likely to make for easier understanding later. For the reasons for the covert sentimentality of Hemingway and the overt lusts of *The Naked and the Dead* are unlikely to be fully understood unless a little is known of the puritan strains brought from England by Anne Bradstreet of Northampton, a poet of uneven attainment but incontrovertible significance; nor is the reason for the extraordinary success of books of the kind and quality of Lloyd Douglas's *The Robe* or Henry Morton Robinson's *The Cardinal* likely to be appreciated unless something is known of the theological traditions of seventeenth-century America.

II

With America as with England there is an acquisition of Norse and Icelandic sagas and legends to begin with; but whether these are a heritage of the abortive colonization of New England by Leif Ericsson in the year 1000, or the more successful institution of the pro-British Giovanni Caboto in 1497 cannot now be established. Nor does it matter; for the myths and epics of Scandinavia, the *Beowulfs* and *Walderes*, remain the same whatever the channel of their translation, and they in turn derive from the even older epics of Virgil and Homer.

Because of the relative lateness of the successful discovery of America by Columbus, verbal story-telling of the kind usually associated with mythology is much less important than theology in American literature. Mythology and minstrelsy are supremely important only when the sole methods of recording stories are by chisel and tablet or pen and parchment. When Columbus set foot in the Bahamas, in 1492, printing was already a flourishing industry in Europe and Peter Schoeffer's three-colour Mainz *Psalter* was more than thirty years old.

The English had been, for them, conspicuously slow in plundering and colonizing the New World. Drake made his raid on the Spanish treasure train in the West Indies in 1572 and later brought back to England the sad survivors of Raleigh's abortive colonization of Virginia; but it was the adventurous John Smith of Lincolnshire who established the first permanent English settlement on what is now Jamestown Island, Virginia.

Having once established a foothold in the new country the English began to emigrate on a big scale, taking their disputatious theologies with them. John Smith was a lusty Elizabethan soldier and a good churchman at heart, like the thousands of eponymous Englishmen who followed him. So were the Puritans who landed in 1620 and the Cavaliers who preceded and pursued them to found the famous First Families of Virginia, though they argued their ways to God along roads that had thus far led only to religious persecution. The point is, that they—plus, by now, William Penn's Quakers and the Dutch expeditionary forces' Calvinists—were truly colonizing: they were establishing those parochial traditions that are the lifeblood of literature.

If the geographically cosmopolitan origins of the invading forces were important their laws and their languages were no less so in the establishment of American literature. It is pertinent to note that there is no indigenous American law: the principles of the established common law are those of seventeenth-century English common law and ancient Roman law. The Roman idea of justice will later be seen to be important: it influences particularly the literatures of the south (Louisiana) and the west (New Mexico), territories in which the invading forces were originally French and Spanish.

The development of printing had a fortuitous influence on American literature. The first printing was done on a press imported from Cambridge, England, and set up in Cambridge, Massachusetts, where it was sponsored by Harvard College, recently founded. For a time printing was confined by law to Cambridge, Mass.; but the nucleus of the industry was subsequently transferred to Philadelphia, and it was here that Benjamin Franklin was apprenticed as a printer and later founded the *Saturday Evening Post*, which continues to this day—though in a form somewhat different from the original. The degree of importance of Franklin's writings will presently be seen.

The writing of several clergymen of the century preceding Franklin's is of small literary importance but had much to do with the paradoxical blending of intolerance and indulgence that is characteristic of America today.

Roger Williams, founder of Rhode Island, was a puritan freethinker with democratic ideas anticipating Whitman's by some two hundred years. The individualism for which Williams fought in his most famous pamphlet, *The Bloody Tenent of Persecution for cause of Conscience*, was entirely religious:

> It is the will and command of God that a permission of the most Paganish, Jewish, Turkish, or Antichristian consciences and worships, be granted to all men in all Nations and Countries: and they are only to be fought against with the sword of God's spirit, the Word of God

while Whitman sang songs of fraternal love and an uninhibited and paradoxically spiritual sensuality; but both loathed oppression and convention. Whitman may have read Williams; but such a conjecture is unimportant. What is important is the realization that Williams set in motion the planet of freedom that soared from the seventeenth-century universe of orthodoxy and reached its apogee with Whitman's strident lustiness.

Increase Mather and his son Cotton were given to witch hunting. Though they sought witches in a more literal sense than does Senator McCarthy the ideas of the latter might be traced by the curious to the writings of the former. Increase was forced to resign his presidency of Harvard after assisting the notorious Salem persecutions. Cotton was an ascetic of brilliant but circumscribed intelligence whose *Ecclesiastical History of New England* is the *vade mecum* of the subject. Both he and his father excelled as keepers of the puritan conscience in a new world that for them was already festering with religious toleration.

Nathaniel Ward, another puritan clergyman, who lived in Boston for a dozen years, wrote an intolerant plea for the pure life in *The Simple Cobler*. In this case the interest lies not in the matter, which was far more thunderously and effectively protested by the Mathers, but in the manner. Ward's literary style was pretentious and alliterative and had a lamentable tendency to jingle within; but he anticipated the demand of the later age of the common man for the coining of phrases and words:

> Tolerations in things tolerable, exquisitely drawn out by the lines of the Scripture and the pencil of the spirit, are the sacred favours of truth, the due latitudes of love, the fair compartments of Christian fraternity: but irregular dispensations, dealt forth by the facilities of men, are the frontiers of error, the redoubts of schism, the perilous irritaments of carnal and spiritual enmity.

Apart from these passionate clerics only one prose writer of the seventeenth century is important, and he for the reason—horrifying enough to the puritans—that he was a sensualist. This was the same John Smith who colonized Virginia.

Smith was a romancer in the traditional English, adventurous, sense. He told stories of the battles he had been in, of his life as a slave in Constantinople, of his capture by Chickahominy Indians and of his explorations of Chesapeake Bay—all of them substantially true but elaborated by the lively imagination of a lusty Elizabethan adventurer who probably had little use for the fabulous embroideries of Sir Philip Sidney's *Arcadia* but absorbed the sensuous beauties of the style of that interminable work and imposed on them the sense of form of the natural writer. It is easy to detect a link between the highly coloured stories of John Smith, which are not now read, and those of a later romanticist, James Fenimore Cooper, which are.

There were three seventeenth-century poets—two of them colonial—whose work has, in small quantity, endured for differing reasons.

Anne Bradstreet's natural Elizabethan lyrical talent was forcibly contained within the inhibitions of puritanism and too often wasted itself in bathos:

> 'Mongst hundred hecatombs of roaring verse,
> Mine stands bleating before thy royal hearse

and in the contentious nonsense of *The Constitutions* in which the four elements argue for supremacy. But she was also capable of—

> If ever two were one, then surely we.
> If ever man was lov'd by wife, then thee;
> If ever wife was happy in a man,
> Compare with me ye women if you can.
> I prize thy love more than whole Mines of gold,
> Or all the riches that the East doth hold.
> My love is such that rivers cannot quench,
> Nor ought but love from thee, give recompence.
> Thy love is such I can no way repay,
> The heavens reward thee manifold I pray.
> Then while we live, in love lets so persever,
> That when we live no more we may live ever

and the later *Contemplations* with their magnificent Spenserian lines.

Edward Taylor's works are gaining recognition today mainly because he forbade that they should be published during his lifetime and they were not in fact examined till 1937. His *Meditations* are metaphysical in inspiration, baroque in their imagery:

> Did God mould up this bread in heaven, and bake,
>   Which from his table came, and to thine goeth?
> Doth he bespeak thee thus: this soul bread take;
>   Come, eat they fill of this, thy God's white loaf?
> It's food too fine for angels; yet come, take
> And eat thy fill! it's heaven's sugar cake.

Michael Wigglesworth wrote a ghoulish Calvinistic poem called *The Day of Doom*, two hundred jingling stanzas long, which became a near-fabulous best seller and may be thought of by the cynical as the first Literary Guild Choice. But it is more enlightening to link its immediate appeal, in 1662, with the frequency of its quotation in every century since—often as an object of overt scorn but with surreptitious veneration for its lurid apocalyptic theme in which all the sinners are cast into hell and all the smug sinless, rejoicing in the punishment of their brethren, wallow for ever in a paradise to which the password was Holier-than-thou.

The importance of these three poets lies not in their technical achievements, for they were all imitators and added nothing technically and little aesthetically to the splendours of Elizabethan and Jacobean poetry, but in the insight we get through them into the puritan mind. It might be claimed that the differences of outlook of that small colonial populace are of little significance; and indeed they are when considered in the sweep of literature in the English language. It is enough to perceive that differences existed and were expressed well enough to gain currency in thought that from the end of the seventeenth century began quickly to crystallize into the democratic utterances of Emerson and Whitman.

III

The speed at which the crystallization of America's thought was accomplished was remarkable. At the end of the seventeenth century there were no newspapers or periodicals for the dissemination of ideas among a rapidly increasing population. Knowledge and ideas had to be gathered exclusively from books and sermons—and there were a quarter of a million colonial immigrants whose ideas had to be developed along lines that were necessarily different from those they brought from cavalier and puritan Europe. Within a hundred years the itinerant quarter-million with their English, Dutch, French and German ideas had become a strongly national race of people five million strong, commercially shrewd, wealthy and sophisticated.

The climate favourable for the accomplishment of this extraordinary metamorphosis was created largely by four writers who happily chanced to be articulate enough, and welcome enough, to be able to continue the literature of America along lines of thought as different as those initiated in this newly discovered land by Mrs Bradstreet, Captain Smith and the Mathers.

Those who have become accustomed to the portrayal in hundreds of films and books of the fine old southern gentleman, usually a colonel, who rules his house with a mixture of despotism and compassion and calls for innumerable mint juleps, will find the prototype in Colonel William Byrd. Byrd was born in Virginia of aristocratic cavalier stock and lived all his life in a style befitting his birth. His published works originated in the journals he kept as records of his own tireless observation. In them detail upon detail mounts meticulously up until an elaborate and accurate picture is formed of the life of those days.

Byrd was something more than a reporter, though. His writing shows humour and concern for the affairs of men in other walks of life than his own. His concern is sometimes a little impatient and lacks understanding, as when he is engaged in surveying to decide the boundary line between Virginia and North Carolina and observes that

> The men, for their parts, just like the Indians, impose all the work upon the poor women. They make their wives rise early out of bed in the morning, at the same time that they lie and snore, till the sun has run one third of his course, and dispersed all the unwholesome damps. Then, after stretching and yawning for half an hour, they light their pipes, and, under the protection of a cloud of smoke, venture out into

the open air; though, if it happens to be never so little cold, they quickly return shivering into the chimney corner. When the weather is mild, they stand leaning with both their arms upon the corn-field fence, and gravely consider whether they had best go and take a small heat at the hough: but generally find reasons to put it off till another time.

Thus they loiter away their lives, like Solomon's sluggard, with their arms across, and at the winding up of the year scarcely have bread to eat.

His misunderstanding, which was common among the Virginia aristocracy, would be brought home to his heirs, for he was writing of men amongst whom were ripening the seeds of discontent that were to come to fruition in the civil war.

But he is a polished stylist whose writings were influential in bringing to notice the simple fact that 'poor whites' existed, perhaps even in originating the sneering generic description 'white trash' and thereby setting the spark to the immense north-south feud that was to be historically investigated with clinical precision by William Faulkner two centuries later in his towering analyses of American decadence.

A romantic idealization of nature that was to influence the clean-living body worship of Whitman and the beautiful nature writing of Thoreau, is to be seen in the work of a French immigrant, Hector St. Jean de Crèvecoeur, whose *Letters From an American Farmer* read today rather like a reminder of a peculiarly American ideal—the back-to-nature cult that has been for generations now a mocking shadow laughing bucolically at the intense pace of city life and exacting payment in the form of a fishing weekend 'away from it all' as the alternative to an ulcerated stomach.

Crèvecoeur was also the first to record the idea of an American nation as a unity to which he and everyone else since Caboto had been contributing:

He is an American, who, leaving behind him all his ancient prejudices and manners, receives new ones from the new mode of life he has

> embraced, the new government he obeys, and the new rank he holds. He becomes an American by being received into the broad lap of our Alma Mater. Here individuals of all nations are melted into a new race of men, whose labours and posterity will one day cause great changes in the world. The American is a new man, who acts upon new principles; he must therefore entertain new ideas, and form new opinions. From involuntary idleness, servile dependence, penury, and useless labour, he has passed to toils of a very different nature, rewarded by ample subsistence. This is an American.

Urban sophistication, bucolic naturalism: to these elements were added the religious mysticism of Jonathan Edwards.

Edwards was the first of the religious revivalists in America, a writer of distinguished prose in which he desired

> to spend my eternity in divine love, and holy Communion with Christ.

He was not the last. The Great Awakening that he originated was later to form an extension of Calvinistic puritanism that was to develop into the aggressive kind of religion that resulted not only in ecstatic manifestations of the Aimée Semple McPherson variety but in the quieter, didactic methodism satirized by Mark Twain and Sinclair Lewis.

Edwards is still held in great reverence—almost as great as the reverence surrounding the work of Benjamin Franklin. The two held opposing views on God—opposing views which have nurtured the toleration that has become in theory the most natural part of American everyday life.

Franklin was to secular life what Edwards was to religious life. Edwards spent his life communing with God and writing of his visionary ecstasies, Franklin spent his life communing with man, with science and with the rationalistic ideas of Swift and Voltaire, and in publicizing those ideas in his *Autobiography* and Addisonian essays. He was the first man to achieve popular greatness solely by his own efforts and in a land shortly to become dedicated to the self-made man he quickly became idolized.

Benjamin Franklin popularized in his writings the very idea of man's humanity to man that the new population needed as an antidote to the religious revivalism of Jonathan Edwards. The people had no desire to be irreligious, but they were beginning to outgrow the practical manifestations of their puritan origins (though puritanism was to retain its hold on their secret hearts right down to the twentieth century) and needed an anchorage for the more materialistic policies necessitated by expansion. It was perfectly easy, whenever it was necessary, to read into Franklin's aphorisms in *The Way to Wealth* far more than the free and individual enterprise he intended. Franklin was a man of action, a go-getter who believed in helping your fellow man first and forgetting to read him a pious sermon afterward. His public services concerned themselves with international diplomacy at one end of the scale and street cleaning at the other. He is the earliest hero of American boyhood. In his writings, as in his everyday life, he gave himself to America; and for this reason his words are as alive today as on the day they were written. Almost the only blot on his literary escutcheon was his attempted revision of the Lord's Prayer to suit the needs of 'today's men and women'—an ill-advised enthusiasm that earned him considerable ridicule even from his most fervent admirers.

CHAPTER TWO

European Influences

I

THE colonization of America coincided with the greatest age of English prose. This fact might have had no greater significance than an influence on the future prose style of American literature; but it happened that the peculiar genius of the early American people was for politics—a science inextricably related to the art of prose and peculiarly dependent on it for success. The ideas of Franklin, Paine, Dickinson and Jefferson were given expression in a prose that had all the power of Renaissance Europe inherent in its traditions. It has proved an enduring prose and reference must be made to it, for without its influences the crystallization of American thought and character into something unique could scarcely have been achieved within the space of a single century.

The Authorized Version of the Bible, mainly the work of Tyndale and Coverdale, is the centre-piece of the magnificent flowering of English prose that succeeded the equally magnificent flowering of poetry and drama of the Elizabethan age. Grouped round the Bible are names that have not since been matched. Broadly, English prose was being wrought by two kinds of writer: those who sought to express their ideas in terms of elaboration, rhetoric and eloquence; and those who needed precision and simplicity. The complex and beautiful phraseology of Robert Burton (*Anatomy of Melancholy*), John Foxe (*Book of Martyrs*), Sir Thomas Browne (*Religio Medici* and *Hydriotaphia*), Jeremy Taylor (*Sermons*) and Richard Hakluyt (*Voyages*) was balanced by those who realized the necessity for absolute lucidity in expounding the theories of science and rationalism. Francis Bacon, though he distrusted English and wrote mainly in Latin, and Milton were the supreme exponents of the art of reducing complex thought to lucid writing.

It would be over-simplifying matters to imply that the sixteenth and seventeenth centuries were remarkable only for the development of antithetical ideas of spiritual experience and scientific experiment and the expression of those ideas in the most superb and varied prose of the whole of English literature. Izaak Walton, for example, is concerned with optimistic enjoyment of the countryside and even the bitterness of the Civil War cannot lure him from his angling and his amiable biographies; and it is Walton who has made the widest appeal to all the generations since his death. But the significance of the fact that the early Americans with their genius for politics fortuitously inherited a prose ideally suited to their purpose cannot be over-emphasized.

The seventeenth century was also the greatest period of English philosophy. The totalitarian ideas of Thomas Hobbes were modified by John Locke, to whose advocacy may justly be attributed the success of the idea of freedom of religious thought that we take for granted today. Locke's political philosophy of the ultimate power of the people was expounded in *Two Treatises of Government*, a work that had a direct influence on the constitution of the future United States. Locke's literary style is dull and often ugly, but there is no doubt of the importance of his influence on American thought.

Inevitably, the newly colonized continent absorbed the ideas of the colonizers; and Europe, from the end of the Middle Ages to the end of the Napoleonic wars, was concerned with swinging an idealistic pendulum from the one extreme of international totalitarianism (represented by the Roman Church) to the other extreme of scientific materialism and Christian Socialism (represented by the philosophies of such men as Rousseau, Hobbes and Locke). But Europe had centuries of feudal complexities to be unravelled; America had only the immediate past to contend with. The embryo nation was fortunate in its era.

II

From the immediate past America took the doctrines that were interesting, examined them and discarded those that seemed useless. A new nation was soon to be brought forth upon the Continent and a new nation can have little use for ideas it believes to be decadent. This apparently logical viewpoint was the one that had to be interpreted and disseminated; and the writers who were most important to that interpretation and dissemination were John Dickinson, Thomas Paine and Thomas Jefferson.

The most important event in America's history was of course the achievement of independence brought about by the Revolution. But the Revolution itself was far from being completely integrated. Its ultimate purpose was the single-minded one of independence; but it was a purpose to a certain extent frustrated by a lack of internal unity. The War of Independence was to be fought against European tyranny, but the additional strife within also demands consideration. It was a strife concerned with the subjugation of colonial aristocracy by the rationalistic socialism that had been so acceptably expressed by Franklin.

As usual, the internal struggle was basically one of wealth against poverty. The wealthy colonial landowners with their Cavalier traditions naturally adopted a policy that was concerned with the preservation of known liberties rather than the establishment of unknown ones. Their philosophy closely parallelled that of the English Whig. But the embryo nation into which Franklin had breathed the sweet scent of democratic freedom was actively radical and cared far less for tradition than for the brave idea of social equality.

John Dickinson wrote from the Whig standpoint and after the Revolution his views were resuscitated and given new expression by the Federalist writer Alexander Hamilton. The literary exponents of radical democracy were Thomas Paine and Thomas Jefferson.

Dickinson was born in Philadelphia. He inherited a fortune, became a very competent lawyer and published a pamphlet called *Letters of a Farmer in Pennsylvania* in which he made clear that he had absorbed many of Locke's ideas. To these ideas he added his own plea for conciliation with England and his idealistic conception of an American empire. His writing is clear, dignified and without spleen: he sincerely holds firm to the belief that the true object of government is the protection of property:

> Let these truths be indelibly impressed on our minds—that we cannot be happy without being free—that we cannot be free without being secure in our property—that we cannot be secure in our property, if, without our consent, others may, as by right, take it away—that taxes imposed on us by parliament do thus take it away—that duties laid for the sole purpose of raising money are taxes—that attempts to lay such duties should be instantly and firmly opposed. . . .

but he has also acquired some of Locke's genius for compromise and moderation: he clearly sees the potentialities of future distress in the radical desire for immediate happiness at little cost:

> Honor, justice, and humanity call upon us to hold and to transmit to our posterity that liberty which we received from our ancestors. It is not our duty to leave wealth to our children; but it is our duty to leave liberty to them. No infamy, iniquity or cruelty can exceed our own if we, born and educated in a country of freedom, entitled to its

blessings and knowing their value, pusillanimously deserting the post assigned us by Divine Providence, surrender succeeding generations to a condition of wretchedness from which no human efforts, in all probability, will be sufficient to extricate them.

The important writings of Alexander Hamilton came at a later date. They stemmed from the same basic ideas but were less moderate in tone.

Hamilton was a Scotsman who became an American citizen and Statesman and Aide to Washington and is remembered chiefly for the *Federalist* papers, a collection of brilliant political writings of which he wrote two thirds. He was an extreme aristocrat by nature and had a fervent hatred for the common people. It was Hamilton who made the famous remark 'The people! The people is a great beast!' And he was concerned at all times with frustrating the radical democracy.

But although Hamilton held the radical democratic idea in contempt his contribution to American political thought was a sound and important one: for he clearly saw the fundamental differences between a democracy and a republic. Actually it was Hamilton's co-author of the *Federalist* papers, James Madison, who expressed the distinction, 'In a democracy the people rule in person; in a republic, through representatives,' but Hamilton continually expounded the common-sense view that a larger territory can be governed by a republic than by an unwieldy mob of self-interested persons.

The writers of the opposing faction were considerably more impassioned but less practically experienced.

Thomas Paine never became an American citizen—indeed he never had the chance, for he had the anarchic knack of saying too many unpopular things at ill-chosen moments and spent much of his life fleeing the fury of France (during the Reign of Terror) or America (for his attacks on Washington and Christianity). He was the son of a farmer of Thetford, Norfolk, and became a Civil Servant in the Excise department only to find himself sacked for agitating for reforms. Franklin, on a visit to London, gave him letters of introduction to friends in Philadelphia and Paine went immediately.

He arrived in 1774 in the midst of the bellicose political confusion that was to lead in a few weeks to the firing of the first shots of the War of Independence. It was an ideal time for an idealistic agitator to begin work. He began. Later, after the confusion had died and independence of a rickety kind had been achieved, he was to be scorned as 'the filthy infidel Tom Paine.' This was because he saw clearly to the heart of a problem and wanted to anticipate the ponderous movements of history by tearing down the feudal barricades of tradition too quickly for slower thinkers; also because he had no discretionary sense at all and acquired none of the statesmanlike diplomacy of Rousseau, with whom he had much in common.

Paine's literary method was very similar to that of the popular-press journalist of the mid-twentieth century: he appealed to the emotions first and the reason afterward. He was a great coiner of phrases that had the simplicity of great eloquence behind them. 'We have it in our power to make the World over again.' 'I thank God that I fear not'—there is a familiar ring today in such Churchillian pronouncements. Paine never in any circumstances used obtuse arguments or windy sentences. All he wrote was simple, clear and bold, unashamedly for popular consumption and immediate appeal:

> These are the times that try men's souls. The summer soldier and the sunshine patriot will, in this crisis, shrink from the service of their country; but he that stands it *now*, deserves the love and thanks of man and woman. Tyranny, like hell, is not easily conquered; yet we have this consolation with us, that the harder the conflict the more glorious the triumph. What we obtain too cheap we esteem too lightly: it is

dearness only that gives every thing its value. Heaven knows how to put a proper price upon its goods; and it would be strange indeed, if so celestial an article as FREEDOM should not be highly rated. Britain, with an army to enforce her tyranny, has declared that she has a right not only to tax but 'to bind us in all cases whatsoever,' and if being bound in that manner, is not slavery, then is there not such a thing as slavery upon the earth. Even the expression is impious; for so unlimited a power can belong only to God. . . .

I have as little superstition in me as any man living, but my secret opinion has ever been, and still is, that God Almighty will not give up a people to military destruction, or leave them unsupportedly to perish, who have so earnestly and so repeatedly sought to avoid the calamities of war, by every decent method which wisdom could invent. Neither have I so much of the infidel in me, as to suppose that He has relinquished the Government of the World and given us up to the care of devils; and as I do not, I cannot see on what grounds the King of Britain can look up to Heaven for help against us: a common murderer, a highwayman, or a housebreaker has as good a pretence as he.

And there is an eloquence directly traceable to the Authorized Version in such a ringing exordium as 'O! Ye that love mankind! Ye that dare oppose not only the tyranny but the tyrant, stand forth!'

Literary history is concerned with Thomas Jefferson, who was to become third President of the United States, mainly because he wrote the Declaration of Independence, the opening sentences of which have become as familiar in quotation as the Gettysburg address:

We hold these truths to be self-evident, that all men are created equal, that they are endowed by their creator with certain unalienable rights; that among these are life, liberty and the pursuit of happiness. That to secure these rights, governments are instituted among men, deriving their just powers from the consent of the governed. That whenever any form of government becomes destructive of these ends, it is the right of the people to alter or abolish it, and to institute new government, laying its foundations on such principles and organizing its powers in such form as to them shall seem most likely to effect their safety and happiness.

These are the theories of John Locke put into language that the mistrals of twentieth-century American creative rhetoric have proved to be corruptible; but like good crystal it had a beauty of its own that lacked only the endurance of the diamond.

III

The valuable part of the American literature of the eighteenth century, then, consisted in writings that were almost exclusively political, written by men whose natural genius lay in that direction and who had fortuitously entered history at a time when the prose on which they perforce had to model their own was at its brightest noonday glory. It was a mighty strength, a marvellous transfusion in which to communicate the power of a new nation. This is not the place to discuss tyrants or tyrannies, but it is not inept to point the poetic justice of the fact that the new continent was able to express its independence in language marked by the noblest literary influences of that other continent from which it so bloodily seceded.

The inheritance of a language that had been wrought into its finest prose shape by Burton and Sir Thomas Browne, by Milton and Walton and Hakluyt, by Bunyan and De Foe and the Bible, at the moment when prose could best serve the needs of history, was not entirely without dangers. It will be seen later that the literature of America has become a self-conscious one largely because the beauty of an inherited language has been made to serve purposes which a rougher product might sometimes have better suited. A nation's literature is born of that nation's anguish and travail and it is not wholly good that the language should be already there, annealed in another furnace and brought forth in its noblest form, for a literature is easier corrupted when it is not in step with a nation's growth and language.

But although the intrinsically valuable part of American eighteenth-century literature is entirely political it is important to discover, toward the end of those anguished years, the embryo of a creative literary art—important because, although a utilitarian literature naturally serves a valuable historical purpose, it is imaginative art that nourishes a nation's spiritual development and is in turn nourished by it, in cycles of decadence and renascence, to the end of a civilization.

The turmoil of the revolutionary years, coming so early in America's modern history, could scarcely be expected to produce much creative literature. Nor did they. But the embryo can be seen quite plainly.

Of drama there was no sign at all—indeed anything approaching a unique American drama was not to appear for many years. The only theatres were in cities occupied by the British and in any case, during the war years public amusements were forbidden. The few stage works that had been written were crude and imitative. To Thomas Godfrey's *The Prince of Parthia* goes the dubious honour of being the first American tragedy to be professionally performed; but the play is without interest, as are the rest of the satires and lampoons that were written and occasionally surreptitiously performed during the war years.

Nor is there any sign of the emergence of an imaginative prose of any unique consequence toward the end of the century.

But in poetry there is something worth a little consideration.

This is the work of Philip Frenau, a New Yorker of Huguenot origin. Frenau was a successful minor poet of three *genres*—the satiric, the lyric, and the horrific. In satire his most successful poem was a long and bitter tirade called *The British Prison Ship*; in lyric perhaps his best achievement was the mildly wistful *The Wild Honeysuckle*:

Fair flower that dost so comely grow,
  Hid in this silent, dull retreat,
Untouched thy honied blossoms blow,
  Unseen thy little branches greet:
No roving feet shall crush thee here,
No busy hand provoke a tear.

By nature's self in white arrayed,
  She bade thee shun the vulgar eye,
And planted here the guardian shade,
  And sent soft waters murmuring by;
Thus quietly thy summer goes,
Thy days declining to repose.

Smit with those charms, that must decay,
  I grieve to see your future doom:
They died—nor were those flowers more gay,
  The flowers that did in Eden bloom;
Unpitying posts and Autumn's power
Shall leave no vestige of this flower.

From morning suns and evening dews
  At first thy little being came:
If nothing once, you nothing lose,
  For when you die you are the same;
The space between is but an hour,
The frail duration of a flower.

But in *The House of Night*, a long and crude Gothic fantasy about the death of Death, with its occasional lines of considerable imaginative power:

Mist sat upon the woods, and darkness rode
In her black chariot, with a wild career

may be seen the anticipation of the morbid investigations that were to be conducted by Poe with such scrupulous nerve-prodding that literature in general and American literature in particular never quite recovered from the induced jitters of soul torment.

Another of the important ramifications of American writing can be traced to these turbulent days. In 1760 some religious verses by a man called Jupiter Hammon were published; not long after came the elegist Phillis Wheatley. Neither they nor their works were in any way remarkable; but both of them were negroes and both were slaves. They were the first to speak for the countless generations of their noble race who were to follow. A negro literature had been established—insecurely, for life itself could only be insecure at this time, but none the less begun.

CHAPTER THREE

Emergence of a National Literature

I

ALTHOUGH in retrospect it is simple to select a date, a name, a title, and refer with didactic glee to 'the first American novel' or 'the point at which the umbilical cord joining American literature to the mother-body of European was severed' there is little pleasure and less profit to be gained from such hack pronouncements. One selects names and titles and dates for convenience' sake, but there is a danger in over-simplification: it is the danger of putting the cart before the horse, of forgetting the background that produced the literature. There is no chicken-or-egg choice in art; it is always the life that produces the art, never the other way round.

The background from which the unique American literature was to materialize was tumultuous enough in its nature and protracted enough in its period to allow little simplification. The fifty years of tumult were over by 1800 and during the next decade there was an interregnum in literary affairs which may conveniently be used as a vantage point of summary.

A climate of tumult tends naturally to produce in the creative field of literature works that are fervidly patriotic—patriotic in a more general sense than that of the political writings, which dealt with different aspects of patriotism. Frenau's poetry sometimes trembled on the verge of sentimentality in its intended bitter gunning against England and thereby lost the sting of its satire; and another work of foundationary importance, Joel Barlow's *Vision of Columbus*, often fell from the epic visionary heights of its intent to a *Land of Hope and Glory* sentimentalizing that is as glutinous as it is dull. It is none the less worth noting that the self-conscious moralizing and the smug visionary look on the face of much contemporary American big-business advertising is not essentially different from Barlow's platitudinizing—though the earlier writer was at least sincere in his search for a native idiom.

So much eighteenth-century American literature had been religious, descriptive, political, philosophical or journalistic that the Addisonian essay and the extended piece of fiction were almost lost beneath the sheer weight of the literature that was busily recording the carving of the American from the European; but right at the end of the century there is a novelist whose work is rather more than a mere literary curiosity.

Charles Brockden Brown spent his Philadelphian youth determining to make literature his profession. In support of his determination he drafted three Virgilian epic poems and read the classics to saturation point. In a country in which there was really no literary profession to enter—the small demand for imaginative literature that existed being readily satisfied with novels imported from England—Brown did remarkably well. He was, it is true, forced to become a lawyer to supply the basic necessities of life; but law was never anything but a spare-time occupation. The rest of his brief life (he was only thirty-nine when he died) he devoted to literary hack work—to 'ghosting' anything that came his way, editing *The Literary Magazine*, and entertaining himself by writing four novels that indicated a new path for American imaginative literature.

The American novels that existed at the end of the eighteenth century were fading carbon copies of Richardson or Sterne or of the floridly elegant novelists against whom those two giants reacted. All of them were didactically moral and appallingly sentimental. C. B. Brown successfully irrigated the new but already arid land of American prose fiction by bringing in the tributary of Gothic horror and romanticism newly discovered in England by Ann Radcliffe and setting it in a genuinely American landscape. He demonstrated in *Wieland* and *Ormond* that disembodied voices, religious mania, mysterious death, and the ghastly clinical details of such diseases as yellow fever were the crude ingredients that his readers needed as an antidote to so much philosophical thought and political theory.

Haste and the pressure of hack chores prevented Brown from fully realizing his intentions and both his style and his plots are often amusingly crude; but his subject-matter proved immediately entertaining. His were the first novels in which American thought, popular appeal and native background were successfully fused. They were also the first American literature of any kind in which a particular emphasis was laid on the rights of women—an interest Brown probably absorbed by reading the works of William Godwin and Mary Wollstonecraft.

With the establishment of a body of fiction that indicated a breakaway from influential models the elements of a complete literature, excepting only drama, could be identified in America. The operative phrase to remember when thinking of that literature as an entity is 'popular appeal.' From now on, the communication to the masses of the tenets of an American way of life, as distinct from any other way of life, became essential. The way of life had been prescribed in literature and established in blood on venues of battle from Concord to Yorktown: it was to be the pen that reinforced the successes of the sword, just as it had initiated them.

II

The few literary magazines that existed in the early days of the nineteenth century were healthily impatient about the emergence of the national literature. In 1805 *The Monthly Anthology* asks categorically: 'Where can we find a single poem of distinguished excellence, or one which will be read fifty years hence? In literature we are yet in our infancy; and to compare our authors, whether in prose or poetry, to those of the old world, can proceed only from the grossest ignorance, or the most insufferable vanity.' Two years later there is a continuing dissatisfaction expressed in the same journal: 'American literature is not a tract where we expect any regular annual product, or where we are sure of constant improvements from the hand of well-directed industry; but it is rather a kind of half-cleared and half-cultivated country where you may travel till you are out of breath, without starting any rare game, and be obliged to sit down day after day to the same coarse, insipid fare.' In the same year *The Select Review* carried an article by Washington Irving in which the operative phrase was 'The man of letters is almost an insulated being, with few to understand, less to value, and scarcely any to encourage his pursuits'; and *The Port Folio* continued its spinsterish twittering: 'Literature languishes in a most inglorious and disgraceful obscurity, because men leave in cold neglect every liberal pursuit; because of avarice in the tutelary power of the country; because we are distracted by feuds and factions of the most rebellious and virulent character; because our modes of education are shamelessly and egregiously deficient; because Classical learning is in the lowest repute; because we have not a national university with all the endowments of an Oxford; and lastly, because the Government itself is inauspicious to the notaries of the muse.'

Such pronouncements may seem to have the irritation of an unjustified impatience behind them; but the impatience itself was an emerging characteristic of the native American. All the world had its literatures and America must have hers too. A hundred and fifty years later we find that the intense and self-conscious desire to conform has been directed inward upon the national character and that in every walk of life a strict conformity to current usage or jargon or habit is the order of things. Every eccentricity of non-conformity quickly becomes in itself a new fashion to be exploited to the death, with the arts naturally reflecting the trends of life.

But in the early 1800's this awareness of the poverty of native literature was a sign of sharpness of mind.

The importance of the investigation of native legend as well as the establishment of American locale was quickly realized. The War of Independence was over, but the war of 1812 was already in the offing. In the lull between the two wars there was bound to occur a reaction from the harsh realities of life; and the reaction was a fully fledged one toward Romanticism. Romanticism—in the historic sense of the Romantic Movement—was already established in Europe. A steady increase in the power and wealth of the middle classes was already apparent and their vicarious idealism was reflected in the immense popularity of writers like Scott and, later, Byron.

The Romantic Movement spread quickly across the Atlantic and Scott and Byron had numerous but unimportant imitators. What was important was that the Romantics, ever mindful of the growing harshness of urban civilization had had recourse to the simplicities of life they believed were to be found in nature and in the simple lives of people who lived 'near to' nature.

> Humble and rustic life was generally chosen, because in that condition the essential passions of the heart find a better soil in which they can

attain their maturity, are less under restraint, and speak a plainer and more emphatic language.

The words are Wordsworth's and belong to another occasion (he is prefacing the Lyrical Ballads) but they fit the present one admirably. The common man, the simple man—the tenets for his understanding had been laid down by Franklin; for a while now they were to be equated with rules for the understanding of Nature; and Nature and Man were to be exploited together in a land of agrarian opportunity.

William Cullen Bryant is the first American nature poet to attain any stature. His poetry is imitative of Wordsworth's in the sense that all nineteenth-century nature poetry is to some extent in Wordsworth's debt. But Bryant's panorama is essentially American: his sunlight, his birds, his flowers, his landscapes are remote from England in words as well as in linear distance; and his particular care is the expression of nature's calming influence on troubled humanity:

> Stranger, if thou hast learned a truth which needs
> No school of long experience, that the world
> Is full of guilt and misery, and hast seen
> Enough of all its sorrows, crimes, and cares,
> To tire thee of it, enter these wild woods
> And view the haunts of Nature. The calm shade
> Shall bring a kindred calm, and the sweet breeze
> That makes the green leaves dance, shall waft a balm
> To thy sick heart.

In many of his poems Bryant is also the upholder of the romantic idea of freedom inspired by the mythological hero of war; and in poems like *The Death of the Flowers* and *A Lifetime* he is enslaved by a wistful nostalgia. Even worse, his elegies are often spoilt by the dullest kind of pretentiousness, as in the opening lines of *The Flood of Years*:

> A mighty Hand, from an exhaustless Urn
> Pours forth the never-ending Flood of Years

—an image unfortunately reminiscent of a barmaid in a cosmic buffet. But nearly all his nature poetry has an enduring quality of minor greatness.

In romantic prose James Fenimore Cooper is the first writer to integrate his stories with the peculiarly American scene. In the sense that his best characters are studies of Indians his romanticism is concerned with the near-to-nature belief.

Cooper's appeal was immediate, for his was the authentic national literature the magazine essayists had been bemoaning the lack of. Woodsmen, pioneer settlements and Indians were his earliest memories and he was a naturally good observer. The plots were unimportant, for Cooper was able by his natural talent to arrange for the suspension of the reader's disbelief for the duration of a full-length novel and beyond, and he was expert in the handling of elemental conflict and physical action. Also, he was capable of writing remarkably dignified and moving prose, as when he describes the death of the fabulous Leather-Stocking in *The Prairie*:

> The trapper was placed on a rude seat, which had been made, with studied care, to support his frame in an upright and easy attitude. The first glance of the eye told his former friends that the old man was at length called upon to pay the last tribute of nature. His eye was glazed and apparently as devoid of sight as of expression. His features were a little more sunken and strongly marked than formerly; but there, all change, as far as exterior was concerned, might be said to have ceased. His approaching end was not to be ascribed to any positive disease, but had been a gradual and mild decay of the physical powers. Life, it is true, still lingered in his system; but it was as if at times entirely ready to depart, and then it would appear to re-animate the sinking form, reluctant to give up the possession of a tenement that had never been corrupted by vice, or undermined by disease. It would have been no violent fancy to have imagined that the spirit fluttered about the placid lips of the old woodsman, reluctant to depart from a shell that had so long given it an honest and an honorable shelter.

His body was placed so as to let the light of the setting sun fall full upon the solemn features. His head was bare, the long, thin, locks of grey fluttering lightly in the evening breeze. His rifle lay upon his knees, and the other accoutrements of the chase were placed at his side, within reach of his hand. Between his feet lay the figure of a hound, with its head crouching to the earth as if it slumbered; and so perfectly easy and natural was its position that a second glance was necessary to tell Middleton, he saw only the skin of Hector, stuffed by Indian tenderness and ingenuity in a manner to represent the living animal. His own dog was playing at a distance, with the child of Tachechana and Mahtoree. The mother herself stood at hand, holding in her arms a second offspring, that might boast of a parentage no less honorable than that which belonged to the son of Hard-Heart. Le Balafré was seated nigh the dying trapper, with every mark about his person that the hour of his own departure was not far distant. The rest of those immediately in the centre were aged men, who had apparently drawn near to observe the manner in which a just and fearless warrior would depart on the greatest of journeys.

Such scenes were to become part of the common heritage of American literature, and, mingled with more idyllic writing would extend the base on which the structure was quickly being built.

III

Although the colourful romances of Cooper offered the vicarious excitement of the backwoods to the rapidly increasing urban population who were unlikely ever to meet with greater adventures than befell them in the founding of fortunes and families, there was a need for another kind of corrective to the growing urgency of city life: the corrective of satire.

Washington Irving was the first of the American satirists. He was also the first writer of American imaginative literature to achieve contemporary fame as an American in Europe. A New Yorker himself, he found in that small but cosmopolitan city ample material for his best works—*The Salmagundi Papers, A History of New York*, and the three books of sketches, *Sketch Book, Bracebridge Hall* and *Tales of a Traveller*. Later, Irving was to develop into a writer of boring travelogues and sententious biographies; but his early work is a delight.

Irving's satire was of the gentlest kind and had a pronounced vein of nonsense running through it. Modelling the essays of *The Salmagundi Papers* on Addison and Goldsmith, Washington and his brother William achieved a great success with their publication in 1807. In 1809 followed the *History of New York*. This was carefully timed to burst its sprightly bubble among the citizens of New York after some carefully planned publicity. The publicity referred to the strange disappearance of one Diedrich Knickerbocker and the discovery among his papers of a manuscript that would be published to defray his debts. Literary hoaxes were new to the citizens, who were completely fooled; but they found Irving excellent value and characteristically rewarded him with an immense regard and immense sales.

The *History* is a pseudo-ponderous work of considerable wit, full of good-tempered caricatures of the Dutch colonists who formed a large part of New York's population. Wouter Van Twiller is one of the best-drawn:

> The person of this illustrious old gentleman was as regularly formed and nobly proportioned, as though it had been molded by the hands of some cunning dutch statuary, as a model of majesty and lordly grandeur. He was exactly five feet six inches in height, and six feet five inches in circumference. His head was a perfect sphere, far excelling in magnitude that of the great Pericles (who was thence waggishly called *Scheno-cephalus*, or onion head)—indeed, of such stupendous dimensions was it, that dame nature herself, with all her sex's ingenuity, would have been puzzled to construct a neck capable of supporting it; wherefore she wisely declined the attempt, and settled it firmly on the top of his backbone, just between the shoulders; where it remained as snugly bedded as a ship of war in the mud of the Potowmac. His body was of

an oblong form, particularly capacious at bottom; which was wisely ordered by providence, seeing that he was a man of sedentary habits, and very averse to the idle labor of walking.

This imaginative, if whimsical, prose of polished and graceful style was an immediate success. Irving's reputation was established in a few weeks. What is more important in a retrospective view, he had set ideas singing in other writers' heads. Within a dozen years he was to find himself writing to a friend: 'Other writers have crowded into the same branch of literature, and I now begin to find myself elbowed by men who have followed my footsteps; but at any rate I have had the merit of adopting a line for myself instead of following others.'

In *The Sketch Book* (including the famous *Rip Van Winkle*) Irving returned to the tradition of the short story, a form he handled with great skill. The plots of his short tales are often borrowed from legendary romances of Gothic origin, but he superimposes his own charming humour on nearly all of them, so that they are always robbed of any macabre feeling and give off a genial warmth instead.

Irving's narrative method is interesting: he invariably uses the apparently slow but carefully organized narration of the *Canterbury Tales*: always there is an establishment of scene and character before things begin to happen, the reader is never bewildered by events that move too fast or by coincidences or surprises; yet the shapeliness of true artistic form is always apparent and it is never spoiled by didacticism of any kind.

Irving's work is not remarkable for profundities or dramatic power; it touches only the fringes of human experience; yet he is worthy of great respect. He was a true and individual American who created a world of fantasy and charm that had international appeal yet remained uniquely American in one particular quality—its humour. Humour is not the whole of literature any more than symphonic form is the whole of music, and for that reason Irving cannot be considered as the first unique American writer; but as a humorist he has been equalled by few and beaten only by Mark Twain; and because the corrective of his gentle irony came at a time of urgency and expansion he is entitled to rather more than mere respect for reflecting and disseminating the inherent humour of a new nation—a humour that might otherwise easily have died in the travail of tumultuous birth.

IV

Bryant's verse, Cooper's frontier romances, Irving's gaiety: the structure is shaping; what is more important, it is shaping with intense individuality. No one had previously seen with a fresh and national eye the American landscape, the American frontier, the emerging American character; and until all these and countless other facets were exposed and polished there could be no whole America on view to the rest of the world.

There was another facet of the American character which now began to emerge: sentimentality. This was bred of an excess of refinement, morality and elegance, which in turn were a reaction against the undertones of war that had sounded for so long in Europe and for a shorter but tenser time in America. Sentimentality (as distinct from sentiment) in overt or introvert form has since become a marked racial characteristic and it accounts for a number of peculiar things in the literature. It is as well, therefore, to be in at its flowering.

There was a hiatus in English poetry from 1830 until Tennyson published his *Poems* in 1842. Keats, Shelley and Byron were actually dead, Wordsworth and Coleridge poetically so; and Tennyson and Browning had as yet achieved nothing. Such a break was aesthetically dangerous

—in America more than in England, where the straws for poetically drowning readers to clutch at came from weathered and substantial ricks.

A few years earlier an insignificant Connecticut recluse, James Gates Percival, had said in the preface to a book of his own sloppy poems, 'Poetry should be a sacred thing, not to be thrown away on the dull and low realities of life. It should live only with those feelings and imaginations which are above this world and are the anticipations of a brighter and better being. It should be the creating of a sublimity undebased by anything earthly and the embodier of a beauty that mocks at all defilement and decay.' This effete shuddering, this reluctance to handle the barge-pole, had no small influence in a period that had few poets of stature. The effusions of elegant poetesses to be found in refined gift books can be an insidious poison, and dilettante ladies did more harm than they knew in circularizing the selections of 'elegant poems from the best authors who adorn the literature of our land'; for their insistence on sentiment and elegance affected even the work of a potentially fine poet like Longfellow.

Sentimental though much of Longfellow's work is, however, there is a sophistication about it which places him far, far higher than the Misses Gould and Brooks and the Mesdames Sigourney and Sarah Helen Whitman, whose chaste piety held the literary public in thrall for many years. It is a sophistication that came from his wide reading and his European travels, and if his character had been a less amiable one it might have etched truth as well as optimism on his best works. But the entire canon of his work teaches the morale of acceptance:

> There is no flock, however watched and tended,
>   But one dead lamb is there!
> There is no fireside, howsoe'er defended
>   But has one vacant chair.

The air is full of farewells to the dying,
  And mournings for the dead;
The heart of Rachel, for her children crying,
  Will not be comforted!

Let us be patient! These severe afflictions
  Not often from the ground arise,
But oftentimes celestial benedictions
  Assume this dark disguise.

He is incapable of harsh thoughts against any man and even the death by fire of his first wife leaves him no more than conventionally moved so far as his poetry is concerned. His technique is facile but slipshod and he has absolutely no sense of reality at all—only a yearning for the picturesque, the refined, the pious. But although he eludes continually the vulgarities of life and attempts to improve on life by shunning its realities, he has an enviable talent for story telling.

It is because of this, because *Hiawatha* and *Evangeline* and all the long narrative poems charm the reader into reading on from line to line simply for the pleasure of discovering what happens next, not for any aesthetic responses in the emotions, that Longfellow has become part of the fabric of American literature. In the sense that he has perpetuated some of the worst characteristics of the Victorian outlook by virtue of the very readability that lodges them in the mind of the reader without evoking any critical faculty, he has been a bad influence. But in the long run no influences can be 'good' or 'bad' to the extent of making or marring a literature. On the other hand, posterity can make or mar a writer's reputation by (*a*) continuing to read him or (*b*) forgetting him and letting him sink into an oblivion beyond resurrection. People are still reading Longfellow.

This of course doesn't make him a good writer; but it establishes a niche for him, and it is a niche in an honourable position. For sentimentality is one of the chief characteristics of American literature and 'the gentle poet of the fireside' saw to its flowering in a way that is infinitely more acceptable than would have been the winsome gushings of the James Gates Percival group.

V

The pastoral element that had so successfully been set in poetic motion by William Cullen Bryant was to be the basis of the work of three other writers, each of whom saw nature in different ways: Ralph Waldo Emerson, Henry David Thoreau and John Greenleaf Whittier.

Whittier came from a Quaker family of New England and his entire output of poems is concerned with three themes—the abolition of slavery, the simple piety inspired by the Quaker creed, and the relationship of the earth to man and of man to work.

His anti-slavery poems are desperately sincere but uninformed by any real knowledge of the problem. He thought of slavery as an abstract wickedness but knew less than nothing about it as a real problem. In consequence his work in this sphere has all the recklessness of diatribe, but none of the elements of genuine conflict. It never becomes more real to the reader than the impassioned yelling of a remote and impotent agitator. Mrs Harriet Beecher Stowe did more for the abolitionist cause in the first year of the publication of *Uncle Tom's Cabin* than Whittier did in twenty years—simply because she reduced the problem to terms of reality in a story that everyone could understand.

But Whittier has a particular skill of his own: he is able to translate into lyric and idyllic terms all that he feels about the spirit of his boyhood New England. He is also much more of a realist than Longfellow: he sees other things besides moral glory in the earthy existence he loves to extol:

> Shrill, querulous women, sour and sullen men,
> Untidy, loveless, old before their time.

He is the apostle of the homespun way of life, his themes are all basic experiences of the human spirit and his settings are all parochial, so that he appeals both internationally and regionally.

Those of his poems that do not deal explicitly with life in rural Massachusetts are deeply religious and usually hymn-like in construction:

> Who fathoms the eternal thought?
> Who talks of scheme and plan?
> The Lord is God! He needeth not
> The poor device of man.
>
> I know not what the future hath
> Of marvel and surprise,
> Assured alone that life and death
> His mercy underlies.
>
> I know not where his islands lift
> Their fronded palms in air;
> I only know I cannot drift
> Beyond his love and care.

Whittier's poetry is technically uneven, often very bad, for his gentle nature concerned itself little with criticism—either of his own or anyone else's work. But it was his work more than anyone's that established the homespun strain that has become a strong feature of American literature and may be found evident today in the work of such writers as Jesse Stuart.

Whittier saw nature as a great organic power with which man must work in harmony; Thoreau is the complete sensualist who is less interested in scientific fact than in philosophical truth:

> Some of my pleasantest hours were during the long rain storms in the spring or fall, which confined me to the house for the afternoon as well as the forenoon, soothed by their ceaseless roar and pelting; when an early twilight ushered in a long evening in which many thoughts had time to take root and unfold themselves. . . . Men frequently say to me, 'I should think you would feel lonesome down there, and want to be nearer to folks, rainy and snowy nights and days especially.' I am tempted to reply to such—This whole earth which we inhabit is but a point in space. How far apart, think you, dwell the most distant inhabitants of yonder star, the breadth of whose disk cannot be appreciated by our instruments? Why should I feel lonely? is not our planet in the Milky Way? This which you put seems to me not to be the most important question. What sort of space is that which separates a man from his fellows and makes him solitary? I have found no exertion of the legs can bring two minds much nearer to one another. What do we want most to dwell near to? Not to many men surely, the depot, the post-office, the bar-room, the meeting-house, the school-house, the grocery, Beacon Hill or the Five Points, where most men congregate, but to the perennial source of our life whence in all our experience we have found that to issue, as the willow stands near the water and sends out its roots in that direction.

He is interested in the spirit of man and is concerned that man should not bother himself with small and unimportant issues. At times Thoreau's apprehension is cosmic in its beauty and his communion with nature is only the means to an end. What he was really concerned with was man's inner life. He saw God at his most divine in the living moment of the present and believed that He would be no more divine if you waited till the end of time. Therefore the good thing was to live the present moment to all the intensity of which the human spirit and the human mind are capable, for the Glory of God. 'I was all alive and inhabited my body with inexpressible satisfaction.'

This intensely pantheistic attitude made Thoreau, so far as is known, a wellnigh completely happy man—anyway during the two years he spent in the log cabin he built with his own hands beside Walden Pond. It was at Walden that he tried the experiment of living without 'getting' a living. The business of getting a living, he contended, always interfered with enjoying life. At Walden he planned so to reduce his hours of work as a handyman that he had ample leisure. He sought a complete freedom from materialism. 'An honest man has hardly need to count more than his ten fingers, or in extreme cases he may add his ten toes, and lump the rest. Simplicity, simplicity, simplicity! I say, let your affairs be as two or three, and not a hundred or a thousand; instead of a million count half a dozen and keep your accounts on your thumb nail. A man is rich in proportion to the number of things which he can afford to let alone.'

Thoreau did not need solitude: he liked to mix with people and indeed was often surrounded by visitors at Walden or was taking part in the normal life of Concord, Massachusetts. Nor was he in the least dewy-eyed about nature—indeed his observations of natural phenomena often have a healthy vulgarity about them. He only sought to live as far as possible without reference to the materialistic standards of life. He considered carefully and with consistent rationality the claims of the machine age, but could see little good in, for example, the new post and telegraph systems if people had nothing of importance to communicate to each other. Like Matthew Arnold and John Ruskin after him and countless humanists before him he forgot that materialism is purely relative and that his observations on communication could clearly be applied to printing or, for that matter, to speech. But he was of course right in defending life against the encroaching industrialization of the machine age which has in fact embraced the whole world to such an extent that material freedom is now impossible and spiritual freedom fast vanishing.

All creative writers are necessarily, to some extent, anarchists. Their anarchic withdrawal from the herd is usually in direct proportion to their imaginative powers, for as soon as they conform to ready-made ideas thrust upon them by convention or tradition they accept the drug of atrophy; and it is a potent drug. Thoreau was the arch-anarchist of all American writers. In his own life he would refuse to take up cudgels to right a wrong, however great, for true anarchy is never aggressive. But he continually signified his disapproval by withdrawal. This dissociation resulted in one of the most important individualist tracts of modern times.

The occasion was the Mexican War of 1846. Thoreau withdrew his support from the government because he saw the war as a blow for the cause of slavery—as indeed it was. The logical extension of his withdrawal was his refusal to pay taxes. He was arrested and imprisoned in Concord jail until his debts were paid for him by relatives. Although this neutralized the effect of his decision it gave him cause to examine the political philosophy of the age and to write in consequence his celebrated essay *Civil Disobedience*.

The document put forward no destructive ideas: it was a closely reasoned analysis of the idea of government:

> Government is at best but an expedient; but most governments are usually, and all governments are sometimes, inexpedient. . . .
>
> This American Government—what is it but a tradition, though a recent one, endeavouring to transmit itself unimpaired to posterity, but each instant losing some of its integrity? It has not the vitality and force of a single man; for a single man can bend it to his will. It is a sort of wooden gun to the people themselves. But it is not the less necessary for this; for the people must have some complicated machinery or other, and hear its din, to satisfy that idea of government which they have. . . .
>
> I have paid no poll-tax for six years. I was put into a jail once on this account, for one night, and, as I stood considering the walls of solid stone, two or three feet thick, the door of wood and iron, a foot thick,

and the grating which strained the light, I could not help being struck with the foolishness of that institution which treated me as if I were mere flesh and blood and bones, to be locked up. I wondered that it should have concluded at length that this was the best use it could put me to, and had never thought to avail itself of my services in some way. I saw that, if there was a wall of stone between me and my townsmen, there was a still more difficult one to climb or break through, before they could get to be as free as I was. I did not for a moment feel confined, and the walls seemed a great waste of stone and mortar. I felt as if I alone of all my townsmen had paid my tax. They plainly did not know how to treat me, but behaved like persons who are underbred. In every threat and in every compliment there was a blunder; for they thought that my chief desire was to stand the other side of that stone wall. I could not but smile to see how industriously they locked the door on my meditations, which followed them out again without let or hindrance, and *they* were really all that was dangerous. As they could not reach me they had resolved to punish my body; just as boys, if they cannot come at some person against whom they have a spite, will abuse his dog. I saw that the State was half-witted, that it was timid as a lone woman with her silver spoons, and that it did not know its friends from its foes, and I lost all my remaining respect for it, and pitied it.

The thought, as can be seen from these three paragraphs, is cogent and smooth. There is no tub-thumping, no panic. And although it could reasonably be argued that a single night in jail is hardly enough to disturb the equanimity of less rational men than Thoreau there is ample evidence that his philosophy was unlikely to have changed even if his imprisonment had been prolonged.

Although Thoreau's policy of passive resistance never had much of a following in America, and even his nature writing seems to be appreciated more in England, he is a vastly important writer in one particular respect: his Civil Disobedience pamphlet was used as the basis of Mahatma Gandhi's mass movement against British Governmental rule. Thus Thoreau is the first American writer whose influence extended to the other side of the world.

As a literary stylist Thoreau has had considerable

influence. His clear, precise sentences and his acute observation are worth the very closest attention. Although he was a romantic—in the best sense—there is a blood-and-muscle reality about such descriptive passages as this:

> To make a perfect winter day like this, you must have a clear, sparkling air, with a sheen from the snow, sufficient cold, little or no wind; and the warmth must come directly from the sun. It must not be a thawing warmth. The tension of nature must not be relaxed. The earth must be reasonant if bare, and you hear the lisping tinkle of chickadees from time to time and the unrelenting cold-steel scream of a jay, unmelted, that never flows into a song, a sort of wintry trumpet, screaming cold; hard, tense, frozen music, like the winter sky itself; in the blue livery of winter's band. It is like a flourish of trumpets to the winter sky.

Later, it will be seen that there is a direct link between the sensuality of Thoreau and that of Whitman.

Thoreau was the first American literary man to record in a fresh and original manner the belief that civilization, in its true meaning, has little or nothing to do with the gadgets that conjure leisure from work and then leave the leisure to be filled by more gadgets so that eventually the human spirit and the human intellect have nothing to do but ascend a spiral escalator leading to universal imbecility. It was given to him, as it is given to all true artists, to perceive and to record his perceptions. The fact that too few people heeded and that the paradox of a world going dotty in the fountain of knowledge has come to pass is beside the point. The world has ever been too enchanted by its own stupidity to pay proper attention to the perceptions of its artists.

Thoreau's early life was spent in the household of the third of those writers who had a special relationship to nature: Ralph Waldo Emerson.

Emerson was a minister's son and himself became a minister in his turn; but he was forced to give up his living after the early death of his wife and he travelled to Europe where he met Carlyle and became his friend and disciple. Back in America he became popular as a lecturer and preacher and his popularity outlasted even the furore he caused by delivering a radical lecture at Harvard—a lecture in which he advised students to abandon their beliefs and the dogmas of their various faiths and discover for themselves what God was like.

Emerson was always a lecturer rather than a writer, but he published several volumes of essays and poetry that stated his transcendentalist philosophy. This was a belief in what he called, with a rather regrettable homespun crankiness, the 'over-soul'—a system of spiritual verities that keep mystically in touch with the infinite. He insisted that God is perceivable only through a divine intuition which all men can develop if they go about it the right way. Optimism and self-reliance are the key qualities and both these characteristics loom largely in Emerson's work. His Bostonian provincial background had shielded him from most of the machinations of corruption and the more overt forms of evil, and evil was a force of which he had singularly little knowledge, though he airily paid lip service to a certain apprehension by explaining that a natural compensation of good restores the equilibrium:

> There is no chance, and no anarchy, in the universe. All is system and gradation. Every god is sitting there in his sphere.

It is this refusal to accept any adequate concept of evil that robs Emerson's philosophy of its strength; but as an essayist he has a formidable power. Almost every sentence he writes is wrought with utmost care into paragraphs so powerful that they belie the worth of their content. He has become one of the most quoted of American writers and his epigrams and proverbs have a rhetorical quality that stems from the didactic nature of a lecturer's ability. 'That country is the fairest which is inhabited by the noblest mind,' he thunders, and we imagine him pontificating in all the pulpits of America. His vision of nature is quite out of touch with reality and the few characters who appear in his poems are bloodless and trivial; but his speculations are those of a thinker who recognizes that others are peculiarly suited to deal with everyday problems while he himself is much better fitted to stimulate people to think on a far more cosmic scale. If there is a whiff of condescension in this attitude it is no more than typical of many men whose interests have inhabited a world of ideas rather than a world of people.

In the canon of American literature the main value of Emerson's *Nature* and *Essays* is that they reveal the mind of the man completely and in that revelation lay bare also much that is beyond. He is a writer to go to for problems—never solutions—and for a prose style that is in the main poetic in spite of the sternness of his utterances.

VI

It is easy to forget that contemporary taste does not necessarily see its important figures—literary or otherwise—so sharply defined as later ages see them. The flotsam of twitterers is washed away on the tide with uncommon slowness and it is sometimes a hundred years before the perspective can be clearly seen and the monolithic giants rise cleanly and untrammelled by the twitterers from the shore. The same observation applies to the establishment of genres and trends in literature. It is easy to say from the peak of the following century that at such and such a time the naturalistic or the romantic or the realistic periods began; but in fact of course they did no such thing. Platitudinous as it may be, it does no harm to recall that everything is happening always, that literature is an infinitesimal part of the world's activity and that it is anyway only a method of recording life that must first be lived.

While Whittier, Bryant, Emerson and Thoreau were establishing their romantically idealized views of God, nature and living; while Irving was speaking with the voice of the urban humorist; Cooper was creating a genuine American *milieu* for the genuine American adventurer to live his adventures in; and all of them were bringing about the emergence of a true and unique literature: there were three other writers who furthered that emergence to such an extent that one of the three became the first uniquely American writer of such stature that he can immediately rank with the literary geniuses of the world.

Herman Melville is that writer and he must be considered apart, for his genius was finer and his scope broader than that of the other two, Edgar Allan Poe and Nathaniel Hawthorne; though Poe and Hawthorne come closer to him in stature than any other American writers in the period thus far explored.

Over the hundred-odd years since his death a deal of sensational nonsense has gathered round the legend of Poe's private life. Many quite intelligent people who have read none of the several good biographies that exist imagine Poe as a kind of neurotic Svengali given to orgies of sex, drink and drugs and ending up by falling dead in the street as the result of his squalid excesses. This is not the place to correct erroneous impressions at length, but a few basic biographical facts are necessary.

Poe's parents died when he was only two years old. He was brought up by a wealthy merchant called John Allan, but was never legally adopted by him. For three years he was a pupil at Manor House School, Stoke Newington, London; subsequently he returned with the Allans to America and finished his education at the University of

Virginia. At eighteen he left the University and soon afterward joined the army. Later he was court-martialled and cashiered—an expulsion that he engineered himself—possibly because he was afraid John Allan's second marriage might deprive him of money. There is evidence that he was a gambler and an alcoholic and that his foster father's luxurious treatment had helped to make his character unstable. There is also evidence amounting to proof that his literary executor forged letters in which Poe was exhibited as a satanic monster.

Subsequently Poe lived in Baltimore and through the influence of John Kennedy, a statesman who was also a best-selling but unimportant novelist, he became editor of *The Southern Literary Messenger*. During the term of his very successful editorship, he raised the circulation considerably and his financial circumstances were eased enough to allow him to marry his cousin, Virginia Clemm, thirteen years old (Poe was twenty-seven) and already an embryo invalid.

Poe worked also on the leading American periodicals of the day: *Graham's Magazine*, *Burton's Gentleman's Magazine*, *Broadway Journal*, and on the New York *Evening Mirror*. He tried for many years to found a magazine of his own, but never succeeded—lack of money being the usual reason for his failure.

Virginia Clemm died. Poe himself fell ill. When he recovered he took on a series of engagements as a lecturer; and these lectures were completely successful. He returned to Baltimore, where he collapsed one day in the street and never regained consciousness. There are no records of the cause of his death and no satisfactory explanation has ever been given.

Poe was first and foremost a professional journalist and literary critic. His poetry and short stories have had an extensive influence, but it is an influence that has permeated subsequent American literature principally via the French symbolists—Baudelaire in particular—who were the first to develop the new technique Poe had originated. His criticism, on the other hand, had an immediate and electrifying effect on American literature.

He began with the premise that the object of all art is not truth but pleasure—a premise that may be strongly argued but which has proved of considerable value in the study of the literary aesthetic. In all his reviews and critiques he was devastatingly caustic when the need arose; but his perception was never at fault. His measured fury was a refreshing antidote to the 'cottonwool' school of dilettante dabblers which several times threatened ascendancy during the first half of the nineteenth century. There has been a long line of brilliant American critics since Poe and all of them are in his debt, for it was he who realized that the extraordinarily rapid development of American literature might easily, if no self-corrective were administered, end in a downward rush leading to the brick wall of a premature death.

Although it is true to say that much of Poe's evaluation of current literature proved wrong—he apparently used the vitriol bottle too little rather than too much and many of the writers he praised have sunk into a warranted oblivion—it is also true that he was among the first to recognize the true value of the work of Tennyson, Dickens and Hawthorne.

Poe's tales and poems were so different from anything that had been written before that there was some justification for the fantastic theories that have since attempted to explain away the writing of them—theories that seek mainly to prove that the tales were merely records of Poe's own sadistic and unnatural life.

He explored the shadowy regions of the Gothic setting that Phillip Frenau had touched on in *The House of Night* and elaborated every detail he found there. In the quite mercenary cause of fee-earning he took the most grotesque and necrophagous situations, highlit the sound of every scream and footfall and made the reader sweat just as he himself sweated with the horrible fascination of sheer revulsion.

His poetry (Yeats called him 'Always and for all lands a great lyric poet'), too, deals with the ravages of a black despair that is at the same time as beautiful as the evocations of horror of the tales.

Poe is concerned in the main with three themes in his creative work: guilt, self-pity and ratiocination. In the tales of ratiocination he substituted the climax of solution for the climax of action and thus, extravagant claims apart, may truly be hailed as the inventor of detective fiction. Although there is a verbosity characteristic of the period in many of the tales, this excess of style is confined to descriptive passages. Poe seldom overloads by so much as a single word any sentence in which he aims to prod the reader's nerve with horror:

> One night, returning home, much intoxicated, from one of my haunts about town I fancied that the cat avoided my presence. I seized him; when, in his fright at my violence, he inflicted a slight wound upon my hand with his teeth. The fury of a demon instantly possessed me. My original soul seemed, at once, to take its flight from my body; and a more than fiendish malevolence, gin-nurtured, thrilled every fibre of my frame. I took from my waistcoat-pocket a pen-knife, opened it, grasped the poor beast by the throat, and deliberately cut one of its eyes from the socket. I blush, I burn, I shudder, while I pen this damnable atrocity.

This (*The Black Cat*) is an example of one of the tales of guilt. *William Wilson* is another. Always in these tales a composite self-portrait emerges: the picture of a well-to-do weak young man who is tainted by hereditary madness in some form or other, who is eternally haunted by the death by wasting disease of a palely beautiful heroine.

Although the sphere of Poe's achievement is circumscribed by fairly narrow limits his stature is that of a major artist; for the ramifications of his influence have extended over the whole of the literature of the western world.

VII

The Mathers, father and son, who at the beginning of the eighteenth century had lashed with all their puritan fury at the manifestation of wickedness they called witchcraft, had as one of their fellow self-appointed judges a member of the family of Hawthorne. Salem, notorious for the witchcraft persecutions, had been the New England home of generations of Hawthornes from 1610; and Nathaniel, born in 1804, didn't leave it until ten years before his death. Thus the microcosm of provincial life and heritage was his only study until, late in life, he travelled to England (to become a consul in Liverpool) and Italy; but by then his finest work was already accomplished. Hawthorne was not the kind of writer whose mind is broadened by travel: he found all he needed in his observation of the development of the puritan conscience, which his forebears had diligently guarded for so many years, and in the study of New England provincialism.

It is not true to say, as many have said, that Hawthorne was obsessed by the longing for fame. He coveted a big audience as any self-conscious artist does, and he spent twelve years conscientiously acquiring the technical skill that might give him one. He was only concerned with fame as a just reward for work well done; and there is no sign of spleen in his acceptance of the stillness and smallness of the voice of acclamation that he eventually heard:

> . . . here I sat a long, long time, waiting patiently for the world to know me, and sometimes wondering why it did not know me sooner, or whether it would ever know me at all. . . . By and by the world

found me in my lonely chamber and called me forth—not, indeed, with a loud roar of acclamation, but rather with a still, small voice.

Those twelve years spent in a lonely room in his widowed mother's house in Salem produced many short stories that were published pseudonymously or anonymously in magazines that catered for the popular taste of the day. All the time he filled his notebooks with plans for more stories—very much as a later great American writer, Henry James, carefully charted the direction of his luminous inspirations.

I would like to picture a virtuous family, the different members examples of virtuous dispositions in their way; then introduce a vicious person, and trace out the relations that arise between him and them, and the manner in which all are affected.

Most of Hawthorne's stories are concerned, as were Poe's, with pathos and Gothic horror; but whereas in Poe the pathos is often of the exaggerated order that properly belongs in the sphere of sentimentality, in Hawthorne it is invariably too delicately done to be anything but deeply moving. And again with horror there is an important difference between the two writers: Poe is happy to explore any horrible situation for the sheer pleasure of inducing a chill in the reader's spine; Hawthorne's horror always arises from some searching examination of moral causes and effects. He is a Dostoievsky in miniature.

Essentially a poet who wrote in prose and a man who loved life and wine, laughter and sensuality, Hawthorne remains at heart a sombre artist—whose real concern is with moral values; and in his greatest novel, *The Scarlet Letter*, he achieves a work of universal significance that yet remains peculiarly American in the sense that the Puritan conscience is used as the mainspring to give impetus to an exposition of the conflict between the individual and society.

The germ of the idea of *The Scarlet Letter* is to be found in an earlier short story *Endicott and the Red Cross*. That story has a paragraph about a young woman

> whose doom it was to wear the letter A on the breast of her gown, in the eyes of all the world and her own children. And even her own children knew what that initial signified. Sporting with her infamy, the lost and desperate creature had embroidered the fatal token in scarlet cloth, with golden thread and the nicest art of needlework; so that the capital A might have been thought to mean Admirable, or anything rather than Adultress.

In the novel the woman is called Hester Prynne. She has borne a bastard child—a little girl called Pearl—to a Puritan minister, Arthur Dimmesdale, and is an outcast from her own section of society. But she wins back the respect of her fellow Puritans by humble unselfishness and apparent submission to Puritan moral laws. Secretly, however, she develops a spiritual independence that she cherishes as a retreat from the morality that has spurned her—and delights in the knowledge that this secret wickedness is preferable to the lovelessness of her marriage to Roger Chillingworth, who deserted her and reappears to wreak vengeance on Dimmesdale. The construction of *The Scarlet Letter* is a masterpiece of balance. Dimmesdale, Chillingworth and Hester are creations of a stature fully worthy of the tragic theme that is played out between them. It has the inevitability of the Theban plays of Sophocles, with something of the same recognition of the workings of fate. 'There is no path to guide us out of this dismal maze' says Hester in a moment of near-despair; and when she begs her husband to abandon his bitter scheme of revenge he explains to her:

> By thy first step awry thou didst plant the germ of evil; but since that moment, it has all been a dark necessity. Ye that have wronged

me are not sinful, save in a kind of typical illusion; neither am I fiend-like, who have snatched a fiend's office from his hands. It is our fate. Let the black flower blossom as it may.

The 'first step awry' is of course the anchorage of the story; but we who watch the working out of fate realize that fate was also the instigator of that first step, that the Greeks' idea of fateful inevitability is at least as powerful dramatically as the doctrine of original sin.

With the publication of *The Scarlet Letter* Hawthorne established himself equally with Poe as a writer who took American prose literature to the very edge of its triumphant emergence. His other novels, *The House of the Seven Gables, The Blithedale Romance* and *The Marble Fawn* do not achieve quite the same greatness. The failure is of technique rather than conception, for in none of the three has he been able to detach himself from his theme enough to ensure that he uses the proper technical method. The result is a creaking, crudely constructed plot in each case. Only the single-mindedness of the conception saves each of them from failure. But that bright quality is clearly in evidence.

The Scarlet Letter was published in 1850; Poe's early tales in the 1830's. Less than fifty years before, *The Monthly Anthology* had been goading the American writer to produce something that would have the stuff of endurance and originality in it. The Romantic Movement had supplied the answer. Humour, nature, moral values—all had been fields of experience for the writers who conducted their investigations with the individual American eye: Irving, Bryant and Whittier; Emerson, Thoreau and Cooper; and, towering above them all, Poe and Hawthorne. It was a proud achievement in so short a time. The romantic adventure tale, the gentle satire, the experiment in sentimentality, the communing with an assessment of nature in relation to man: these were important images to be reflected by the mirror of literature. But they would all lose their clarity without the astringent investigation of horror by Poe or the realization by Hawthorne of human tragedy and human nobility. The first half century of the Romantics had gathered to itself an impetus that made nonsense of chronology. From now on the status of American literature was assured for so long as it continued to look around and show the rest of the world the face of America. It had proved that the country had developed a character of its own and that, for example, the frontier tales of James Fennimore Cooper could be read and enjoyed far beyond the parochial limits of their setting, because they made a fundamental appeal to the emotions and at the same time satisfied the curiosity about a way of life that could not exist elsewhere.

All the elements of a fine literature were in fact in evidence by 1850; and a year later was to see the publication of *Moby Dick*, Melville's masterpiece, into which great whole was fused everything that stood for the conflict of the forces of evil against the essential nobility of the human spirit.

CHAPTER FOUR

Cities and Plains

I

HAWTHORNE needed no inspiration beyond that to be found in his native New England. Melville could write no word till he had travelled abroad. An urban New Yorker by birth and an intended schoolmaster by profession, he found neither satisfaction nor security in the life of the growing city and enlisted while still in his teens as a common sailor. The ship was a whaler and the captain something of a brute—though it is easy to forget that tyrannical masters were needed for the crews of those days, as it is easy to forget that Melville's upbringing and inclination of temperament were both too gentle to have fitted him for the rigours of whaling. Anyway, Melville deserted his ship eighteen months after he had joined her, while she was harbouring at Nuku Hiva in the Polynesias and was caught by the Typees, a race of cannibals whose curiosity and friendliness seemed greater than their fleshly needs, for they kept Melville and his fellow fugitive Toby Green in friendly confinement for some months. Then came the opportunity for escape in the shape of an Australian ship that took him away from the Typee valley but not away from the South Seas.

For some months more Melville led an itinerant life among the South Sea islands, working his passage from port to port as the mood took him and deciding, after nearly four years of wandering, to return to New York. He had gathered experiences enough for a lifetime of books and he would tell the world what he had seen.

He could not have chosen a better time. Dickens, on his first visit to America, had aroused a vast literary enthusiasm, and the kind of book Melville chose to write—a more or less factual account of his adventures in the South Seas—was so completely new that it could hardly fail to find a public. Within a few months of its publication *Typee* was a *succès de scandale*, reviewed and praised by Hawthorne and the young Walt Whitman (who was at that time roaming New York) and coinciding with a craze for escape and travel books that Richard Dana's adventure story, *Two Years Before the Mast*, had done much to foster.

Typee was received with shock as well as pleasure because Melville had enlightened his readers on the natural idyllic state of the Polynesian islanders and pulled no punches in his exposition of the way in which that idyll was being shattered by missionary Christians who introduced not only knowledge of Christianity but the ideas of corrupt commerce and—worse—the venereal diseases which hitherto had been unknown. He made very plain his disgust at the 'civilization' that in so short a time could destroy with its vices and diseases the integrity of a whole brave race.

Later, he was to find at the heart of that same civilization a magnificent nobility and to extol it in one of the greatest allegorical works ever to be written.

II

Melville immediately wrote a sequel to *Typee*, in which he continued the narrative of his adventures after he left the cannibal island. *Omoo* too was a success. On the strength of it Melville married Elizabeth Shaw, the daughter of the chief justice of Massachusetts, and made a handsome home for her in New York. The appeal of his two South Sea island books was rapidly becoming more or less world wide and he felt that he could now turn his attention to more serious work.

The result was *Mardi*, a book that tries to be both a popular adventure story and a profound allegorical fable and fails partly on both levels. The failure was in a measure due to a public that felt embarrassed when trapped into spiritual explorations; but in fact Melville had not properly controlled his ideas, and *Mardi* can be considered valuable only as a blueprint for *Moby Dick*.

After the failure of *Mardi* Melville was forced to do some hasty retrenching. He quickly wrote two more adventure stories, *Redburn* and *White-Jacket* and moved into Arrowhead Farm, Pittsfield, planning to supplement his literary income by the sale of farm produce. It was an heroic venture but not one for which Melville was constitutionally fitted: a farmer's life demands far more energy than can be spared by a man whose interests are elsewhere. But if the schism in his life was one that caused mental unhappiness it at least brought about also the conditions of violent unrest in which *Moby Dick* was written.

Hawthorne was Melville's neighbour at Arrowhead. The two writers met and talked often and discussed their problems. Melville tried to explain what had been in his mind when he wrote *Mardi*, how he had wanted to show in an allegory that man's superb qualities were as nothing against the cruelties of nature, against a God who claimed the dove yet made the shark. Yet 'What I feel most moved to write, that is banned—it will not pay. Yet, altogether write the other way I cannot. So the product is a final hash; and all my books are botches.' He was not the first writer to try and compromise between the heart and the stomach and fail in the attempt; nor would he be the last.

None the less, with Hawthorne's encouragement *Moby Dick* was begun and finished, and published in 1851.

Its sales were not enough to cover the pitifully small

advances, a few hundred dollars, Melville had received from his publishers.

The few critics who noticed *Moby Dick* at all thought it was complete nonsense; the rest, and the public, treated it with utter indifference. Melville was already exhausted with the loss of the energy he had expended on the book. Now the bitter disappointment that was none the easier for having been in part expected, left him physically and mentally ill. He determined to begin another 'and even more obscure' book. This was *Pierre*, published in 1852, as a challenge to those who thought *Moby Dick* a nonsensical extravaganza. *The Confidence Man* followed, and, although it was a satire Melville intended to continue, it was in fact the last long book he wrote. Only a few stories (two of them masterly) and essays were to come before this strange genius eventually accepted defeat, gave up writing, and took a job as a civil servant—the final indignity for a man whose marvellous mind should have been lauded across two continents.

Years of distressing poverty and sickness defeated only his body, and, for a time, a little of his brain; his indomitable spirit was still able to conceive the small masterpiece *Billy Budd* and accept serenity in old age. When he died in 1891 a single newspaper published a four-line obituary.

There is of course another point of view to be explained: the probable reason for the public's refusal to accept *Moby Dick* and the works that followed it.

Melville was a metaphysical writer who had in fact little pure technical skill as a craftsman. His reading during his years before the mast had been mainly in the great Elizabethans—Marlowe, Jonson, Burton and the metaphysical Caroline poets. He acquired from them all the food for thought he needed, but none of the constructional skill that might have enabled him to adapt what he wanted to say to a form that would have proved acceptable. After

Moby Dick he began to theorize instead of construct, waving words and styles aimlessly about as if they were veils that would entrance the readers with a kind of hypnosis. But the reading public is not so easily deceived. An absolute genius like Beethoven can break every rule and no one will bat an eyelid; but Melville's genius was not of this order. He sustained it for the length of a single book and then it fell from him with the brittle dryness of autumn leaves. The sap had fallen.

But for the brief span of his achievement in *Moby Dick* he inherited a genius of the very noblest order. The subsequent failure was immaterial; and the assessment of that failure from a critical viewpoint is interesting only for the record.

> The sum and substance of our fault-finding with Herman Melville is this. He has indulged himself in a trick of metaphysical and morbid meditations until he has almost perverted his fine mind from its healthy productive tendencies. A singularly truthful person—as all his sympathies show him to be—he has succeeded in vitiating both his thought and his style with an appearance of the widest affectation and untruth. His life, as we should judge, has been excessively introverted.

The assessment is from a magazine article of 1857, the critic Fitz-James O'Brien. His words can stand for the record. But the masterpiece and its place in literature must be given more consideration.

III

On the face of it, *Moby Dick* is an adventure story of the high seas. Simply as an authentic record of conditions that no longer exist the book is most valuable, for the days of this kind of whaling, this grappling at close quarters with the largest of the sea's creatures, have long been over. And authentic it certainly is. Melville had his own experience of whaling to go on, and in addition he read avidly every book he could find and made full use of the story of the famous Mocha Dick, the white whale who had killed upward of thirty men before being finally conquered in 1859.

The surface tension of the story is achieved through the bitter feud of Captain Ahab and Moby Dick. Ahab has lost a leg in an encounter with the whale and is determined to wreak his vengeance; and to this end he has made his crew take an oath that they too will dedicate themselves to the destruction of the monster:

> I, Ishmael, was one of that crew; my shouts had gone up with the rest, my oath had been welded with theirs; and stronger I shouted, and more did I hammer and clinch my oath, because of the dread in my soul. A wild, mystical, sympathetical feeling was in me; Ahab's quenchless feud seemed mine.

Ahab's attitude to the whale is far stronger than simple hatred in return for an injury:

> The White Whale swam before him as the monomaniac incarnation of all those malicious agencies which some deep men feel eating in them, till they are left living on with half a heart and half a lung. That intangible malignity which has been from the beginning; to whose dominion even the modern Christians ascribe one half of the worlds; which the ancient ophites of the east reverenced in their statue devil; —Ahab did not fall down and worship it like them; but deliberately transferring its idea to the abhorred white whale, he pitted himself, all mutilated, against it. All truth with malice in it; all that cracks the sinews and cakes the brain; all the subtle demonisms of life and thought; all evil, to crazy Ahab, was visibly personified, and made practically assailable in Moby Dick.

There is a superbly handled pursuit of the white whale, in which Ahab deliberately smashes his direction-finding instruments and spurns the words of wisdom of his mate although he knows them to be true. In his anguish and fury he refuses even to go to the aid of a sinking ship. The whale is found and angered and in the climatic battle at the end of the three days' pursuit sinks the ship and ponderously goes his way as the sea engulfs the drowning bodies of the crew.

But this story is merely the dramatic means by which Melville offers his interpretation of life—an interpretation that is strangely profound and marvellously illuminated by variations in style that defy all the rules of coherent drama yet merge into an organic whole.

The allegorical significance of the work seems to have escaped Melville until it was pointed out by Hawthorne, for he wrote to Hawthorne's wife in 1852 and remarked in passing: 'I had some vague idea while writing it that the whole book was susceptible of an allegorical construction, and also that parts of it were—but the specialty of many of the particular subordinate allegories were first revealed to me after reading Mr. Hawthorne's letter, which, without citing any particular examples, yet intimated the part-and-parcel allegoricalness of the whole.' But his surprise is not really remarkable. The writer does not sit down and tell himself 'I am going to write an allegory'; his intentions are usually just to tell his story, and the less conscious he is of any 'significance' attaching to it the better.

But there is no doubt about the 'allegoricalness' of *Moby Dick*. All the races of the world are represented by the crew of the whaler and the sum total of human nature is exhibited in the character of Ahab, just as the monstrous whale is representative of the universal force against which man is eternally pitting himself with the full knowledge that that force is his *raison d'être*. Nor can there be any doubt that with *Moby Dick* Melville achieved a work that ranks with the greatest novels of the world.

There is no failure in *Moby Dick* as a whole and any

attempt to criticize its parts can result only in insultingly small-minded carping. Like a late Beethoven quartet its revelation is on a cosmic scale and it has that unique quality that elevates the mind and heart of the reader to similar cosmic heights. It is also an anticipatory realization of a new polyglot nation coming to terms with life and beginning to understand the smallness and the greatness of man and the simultaneous impossibility and necessity of absolute unity of heart and mind and spirit. In this lies its uniquely American quality.

IV

Romanticism, which as a literary movement is the heightening of the imaginative powers of the writer in order that he may create a world into which the reader will willingly escape, soared to its apogee in the work of Melville and Whitman. But before considering Whitman, the first to glorify the whole American in poetry touched by genius, it must be pointed out that in the work of both these unique Americans there are unmistakable signs of a revolt against Romanticism as well as a glorification of it. Melville chose a *locale* of exotic remoteness for *Typee* and *Omoo* and presented an idealized civilization into which his readers could escape for comfort; but he couldn't resist adding the realistic side of the picture in which he pointed out that both the ideal civilization and the pioneers who mined it with their syphilitic corruption really existed—were in fact the Polynesians and the 'civilizing' missionaries of Europe and America. Likewise, he made *Moby Dick* a magnificent adventure story first and foremost but made quite sure that the symbolic significance of the ocean and the white whale were never touched by the highlights of romantic glorification. Man lives his life in pursuit of death across a sea of universal doom, and the glamour of the moonlit ocean of summer midnight is as transitory as the goodwill of Christmas.

The revolt against Romanticism was later to develop into the twin streams of Realism and Naturalism and it is relevant to note that in 1851 Whitman as well as Melville was thinking in the direction of a counter-Romantic movement:

> A desire that had been flitting through my previous life, or hovering on the flanks, mostly indefinite hitherto, had steadily advanced to the front, defined itself, and finally dominated everything else. This was a feeling or ambition to articulate and faithfully express in literary or poetic form, and uncompromisingly, my own physical, emotional, moral, intellectual, and aesthetic personality, in the midst of, and tallying, the momentous spirit and facts of its immediate days, and of current America—and to exploit that personality, identified with place and date, in a far more candid and comprehensive sense than any hitherto poem or book.

Whitman did not of course write 'in a far more candid and comprehensive sense' than anyone before him. That is a delusion often suffered by writers. They discover truth and imagine—quite innocently—that no one has ever discovered it before them; it is rather as if someone should discover for himself that two and two make four and claim the invention of arithmetic. But the innocent mistake is not important. Truth is continually being re-presented by creative artists and so long as it is re-presented through the unique vision of a fresh spirit the re-presentation will have value.

Whitman's was such a spirit. His best work is concerned with reinterpreting the oldest of the emotions and experiences: war, love, death, beauty. He brings his vision to bear on the aeons' accumulation of these emotions and experiences and his vision is the vision of an American who is deeply proud first of being a citizen of America and second of being a citizen of the world. For the first time he embraces the world with an American love and points to his body with the healthy lust of that strangely paradoxical being, the extrovert poet.

The proportion of Whitman's work that is touched by actual poetic genius is small—far more is merely talented; in this he is like Melville; also, that proportion is nourished by the blood of the counter-Romantic movement:

> Slow-moving and black lines
> creep over the whole earth—
> they never cease—they are
> the burial lines,
> He that was President was buried,
> and he that is now
> President shall surely be
> buried.

The same kind of spiritual motivation urges forward the beautiful poem *Camps of Green*:

> Not alone those camps of white, old
> comrades of the wars,
> When as order'd forward, after a
> long march,
> Footsore and weary, soon as the
> light lessens we halt for the night,
> Some of us so fatigued carrying the
> gun and knapsack, dropping
> asleep in our tracks,
> Others pitching the little tents, and
> the fires lit up begin to sparkle,
> Outposts of pickets posted surrounding
> alert through the dark,
> And a word provided for countersign,
> careful for safety,
> Till to the call of the drummers at
> daybreak loudly beating the drums,
> We rise up refresh'd, the night
> and sleep pass'd over, and
> resume our journey,
> Or proceed to battle.

Lo, the camps of the tents of green,
Which the days of peace keep
filling, and the days of war
keep filling,
With a mystic army, (is it too
order'd forward? is it too
only halting awhile,
Till night and sleep pass over?)

Now in those camps of green, in
their tents dotting the world,
In the parents, children, husbands,
wives, in them, in the old and
young,
Sleeping under the sunlight, sleeping
under the moonlight, content
and silent there at last,
Behold the mighty bivouac-field
and waiting-camp of all,
Of the corps and generals all, and
the President over the corps and
Generals all,
And of each of us O soldiers, and
of each and all in the
ranks we fought,
(There without hatred we all, all meet.)

For presently O soldiers, we too camp
in our place in the bivouac
camps of green,
But we need not provide for outposts,
nor word for the countersign,
Nor drummer to beat the
morning drum.

But if the work of his genius was in small proportion to the work of his talent, his talent is not less important; it is in fact more important, for in the work it produced can be found Whitman's uniquely American quality. In works like *Camps of Green, Ashes of Soldiers* and *To The Sunset*

Breeze Whitman belongs to the world; but when he writes:

> This is the city and I am one of
> the citizens,
> Whatever interests the rest interests
> me, politics, wars, markets,
> newspapers, schools,
> The mayors and councils, banks,
> tariffs, steamships, factories,
> stocks, stores, real estate
> and personal estate,

he protests too much his American interest in mankind and becomes a bore, just as the American of the nineteen-fifties falling over backward in his vigorous denial of the blight of homosexuality—which no one would have suspected him of if he hadn't mentioned it—is boring in the extreme. Moreover it isn't poetry, whether written by Whitman or anyone else. But it is the expression of a self-conscious nationalism glamorized up to the very titles and as such is important, since its sentiments led the America that followed Whitman into a conception of democracy that was both banal and pretentious and was to receive no strong corrective until Sinclair Lewis attacked it with his astringent satire in the nineteen-twenties.

V

Walter Whitman was born on Long Island in 1819. His father was a carpenter who sent him to school in Brooklyn. He began his working life as an office boy and later became a school-teacher, a printer, a journalist and an editor. But his experience was by no means parochial. He travelled a lot within the continent of North America and broadened his outlook in the sense that he learned to love all kinds and conditions of living things—the vegetable, the seed, the animal and the city, as much as man himself. He was superbly healthy in body and mind, and while he travelled and hunted with farmers (and their daughters) he read completely through Scott's poetry, Aeschylus, Sophocles, Dante, Homer and the Bible.

During the time he stayed in New Orleans—it was only a few months—he formed a relationship with a woman who subsequently became his lover and by whom he had one—at least one—child. The details of the liaison are obscure and although he wrote to John Addington Symonds many years later and mentioned a grandson no one has ever stepped forward to claim the relationship.

Very soon after this passionate experience of love he began to write poetry.

Leaves of Grass is really the generic title of the whole of Whitman's work, for it was added to volume by volume until the end of his life. The longest poem in the first volume is entitled *Walt Whitman* and begins

> I celebrate myself.

But it is the whole of mankind that he is celebrating:

> And what I assume you shall
> assume;
> For every atom belonging to me,
> as good belongs to you.
> I am of old and young, of the
> foolish as much as the wise.
> I embody all presences outlawed
> or suffering.

The Emersonian doctrine of rejoicing in the innate goodness of humanity, plus the muscle-and-blood reality of Thoreau's ceaseless observation, form the two main influences in Whitman's work. He believes with all his heart in the nobility of the common man and it is the common man in every phase of his waking, working and sleeping life who peoples the America of the poems. This concentration on the microcosm of the country he loved gives his work a unity that inevitably invites the accusation of monotony; and it is true to say that neither Whitman nor his poems ever changed. He experienced no transitional periods of technical accomplishment. Coming to the business of writing poetry he was already fully armed with the technical equipment that was to see him through to the end of his life. All he had to say he could say in the long-line style that without the inspiration of his moments of genius resembles, and often is, chopped-up paragraphs of prose. He remained always a bad grammarian and a dabbler in too many foreign-language words. It apparently never occurred to him that the sense of a verse could be carried on from one line to another; so he created a new poetic problem for himself—the problem of how a whole sentence designed to be read as one line can be accepted without question by the reader. And it is a problem that is invariably insusceptible of solution. But in his best work—best, that is, poetically—he creates in these long lines a sense of anticipation that arouses satisfaction in the reader, just as a purely metrical line in a verse of Shelley's might arouse satisfaction.

But once again it must be emphasized that Whitman is important not so much for his poetic achievement as for his uniquely American voice. He pitched his songs of fraternal love in the key that was within the compass of all his countrymen—ill-educated and dispersed about a mighty continent though thousands upon thousands of them were. He believed, as Benjamin Franklin had believed, in a free materialistic world full of geniality and beauty, and his songs, and the voice in which they were sung, were just that much louder and clearer and nearer the nerve than Franklin's had been. Also, conditions for the singer of democratic songs were more fruitful than they had been for Franklin: the second great cataclysm in American history, the Civil War, involved Whitman as if it had been waiting for his voice to be added to the abolitionist cause.

VI

Characteristically, Whitman's first thought when the war broke out was for his body:

> *April 16th* 1861. I have, this day, this hour, resolved to inaugurate for myself a pure, perfect, sweet, clean-blooded, robust body, by ignoring all drinks but water and pure milk, and all fat meats, late suppers—a great body, a purged, cleansed, spiritualized, invigorated body.

He was forty-two and he was reluctant to join in the fighting, not because of any physical fear—the thought is laughable—but because of the Quaker tendencies in him which rejected any aggressive soldiering. His younger brother immediately volunteered for service and a year later Whitman was involved as deeply in the war as if he had been fighting himself. His entire mental and physical energies were given over to voluntary work among the wounded and dying soldiers in Washington.

There he stayed for ten years, revolting and at the same time exalting in the sight of agony and death. 'I believe no men ever loved each other,' he wrote, 'as I and some of these wounded sick and dying men love each other.' His services to them, it is true, were of the simplest kind but of immense value: he would take them newspapers and tobacco and read or talk to them and inspire them by his magnetic personality with the will to live.

During all this time his life was a life of self-sacrifice and devotion. He lived in the simplest way so that he could support his family and continue his services to the soldiers. It was a period that naturally produced some of his finest work—work in which little is said of the glory of war and much of its horror. Some of his smallest pictures of a wound or a bivouac or a streak of moonlight illuminating the hand of a dying man in a field hospital are invested with the universal significance of truth; and the reader of the war poems is moved sometimes beyond endurance. Such is the greatness of true art.

VII

With the beginning of the counter-Romantic movement that is integral with Whitman's naturalism it is convenient to draw attention to the fact that the rise of industrialism was the main cause of the move away from Romanticism in American literature.

The great works of Melville and Whitman were concerned scarcely at all with these urban impulses and encroaching ramifications of city life. True, Whitman included city workers in his all-embracing catalogues of people, just as he included places:

> Wait at Liverpool, Glasgow, Dublin, Marseilles, Lisbon, Naples,
> Hamburg, Bremen, Bordeaux, The Hague, Copenhagen,

but one feels that he was being benevolently embracing, like the B.B.C.'s Grand Goodnight in the radio-mad 'twenties, and that it was just the wish not to be thought forgetful rather than any particular love of city dwellers that made him specifically consider them. The same with Melville: he considers mankind as a whole—even more circumambiently than Whitman, for the purlieus of nationalities in *Moby Dick* is no smaller than the whole world—and he was inspired at all times by the spirit of the plain and the ocean rather than the sophistry of the city.

But Whitman, the great all-American, would not have regretted the encroaching tide of industrialism that was gradually reshaping the continent he loved at the very moment of his setting down of the battle pieces of the Civil War. Whitman regretted nothing that followed naturally from America's growth: it was all grist to his mill.

If he had known that in the years 1870–1900 the population of the United States had increased to nearly eighty million he would doubtless have celebrated the increase in a poem. But by 1891 he had died, having truly said of himself:

> I have loved the earth, sun,
> animals, I have despised riches,
> I have given alms to everyone
> that asked, stood up for the stupid
> and crazy, devoted my income and
> labours to others,
> Hated tyrants, argued not concerning
> God, had patience and indulgence to-
> ward the people, taken off my hat to
> nothing known and unknown,
> Gone freely with powerful uneducated
> persons and with the young, and
> with the mothers of families,
> Read these leaves to myself in the
> open air, tried them by trees,
> stars, rivers.

It is, then, to other writers that we must look for the chronicles recording the industrialization of America, the rise of vast cities, and advancing science.

So far as philosophic thought was concerned the main influences came mainly from England. The works of Darwin, Herbert Spencer and T. H. Huxley, for example, provoked American writers to deal controversially with the issue of God and His personal love in an age of scientific realism. And Zola, Tolstoy, Flaubert and Hardy carried realism and naturalism to their logical conclusions along the plane of fiction, sounding their echoes in the American school of fiction that began about 1870 and expanded slowly during the next fifty years. It was an age in which American literature, having reached its peak with Melville and Whitman, was to become inextricably linked with the literature of Europe—a literature of influences that are to be considered in the next chapter.

But it must not be concluded that urban life had an immediate and obvious effect. On the contrary, there was considerable hostility to a school of literature founded on evolutionary thought. People were not so easily made to relinquish their hold on the romantic notions of a movement that had gained remarkable impetus in fifty years. Their taste had to be re-created for them; and writers themselves had first of all to apprehend the reasons for that change.

VIII

The work of Samuel Clemens, pseudonymously and unforgettably known as Mark Twain, belongs to the period following the Civil War, in which the creative artist looked around him and through the mysterious alchemy of his apprehension was able to anticipate the transition that was taking place in the life of his country.

From the literary surveyor's point of view the satire in Clemens's work is more important than the picaresque but parochial humour; the jokes of Tom Sawyer and Huckleberry Finn begin to fade a little now—though the characterization in those remarkable stories set in the Mississippi Valley is as strong as ever; but his irony retains to the full both its sharpness and its vulgarity.

In *The Gilded Age* Clemens is concerned with an attack on the national government and the political corruption that was rife within it; and although the novel itself is a bad one technically (probably the result of a collaboration with an unimportant novelist, Charles Warner) its satire is accurately aimed and significantly effective.

Elsewhere Clemens is guilty of much poor taste—which would not matter if only his own reputation were at stake; but he has acquired such an enormous readership and such an inviolable position in American letters that his vulgarity has had a considerable influence on later satire.

It is unfortunately a vulgarity of the less admirable kind. Subconsciously concerned only with perceiving that Romanticism has reached the stage where it needs a sharp corrective, he chooses to make some uncultured attacks on Scott and on Christian Science—both easily withstanding Clemens's petty diatribes—in *The Innocents Abroad* and *A Yankee at King Arthur's Court*. The idea of finding the weak spots in the chivalric armour of medieval feudalism is a good one; but because he finds the Middle Ages rife with brutal cruelty (which indeed they were, but were not unique in that respect) he includes in his boorish gibes not only the cruelty but the culture too.

Yet in spite of his ill-phrased attacks on Romanticism Clemens could not resist selecting one of the most chivalrous figures of the Middle Ages and holding her up for his own and the public's fulsome adoration. His *Personal Recollections of Joan of Arc* is a vast tableau—most carefully constructed technically—in which Joan appears again and again in the idealized form that is typical of the Romanticist outlook.

Always curiously unstable in both temperament and technique, Clemens in his later work attempted an analysis of human nature that was intended to be Swiftian in its cynicism, but which never really possessed the courage of its convictions. He is important as a satirist because of that very instability. For, like many another writer, he was a barometer needle indicating, before it had actually occurred, a change in the climate of life. And instability was to be a characteristic of that new climate.

The change was largely due to the branching out of journalism which in the last thirty years of the nineteenth century spread in concordance with the rapid growth of cities. Enormous increases in population meant corresponding increases in literacy; but it was a literacy that necessarily had to be equated with the lower standards of education prevailing in the popular schools. From now on popularity was to be a factor of importance, if not an actual criterion, in journalism. New methods of production had resulted from the progress of science; the industry of journalism was well able to cope with the enormous demands of the reading public; it was only necessary for writers to fall in and follow the band, and since their economic problems were much the same as everyone else's they could not afford to demonstrate their reluctance to do so unless they were either independent of their earnings or conscientious enough as artists to look away from the blandishments of a quick but ephemeral success. Similar blandishments are offered today by cinema, radio and television to any writer who is willing to forsake the art of literature for the elementary skill necessary to construct ephemera likely to appeal to an audience seemingly compounded of cretins and guttersnipes. Any writer with any sense will of course take a long view of the position and realize that such media are by their very nature ephemeral; but his economic position too often forces him to ignore the realization.

There were of course the few conscientious artists who held out: one of these, Henry James, will be considered in due course. Also, it would be foolish to imply that the influence of journalism was a wholly bad one: such an implication would be most misleading. There were immense benefits to be gained by the writer from the close contact with his public that journalism demanded; he was forced not only to climb down from the ivory tower in which he may have imagined himself secure, but also to ensure that he had his finger on the public pulse and be able to note and respond to its variations. This meant in effect that he must above all remember to be entertaining. Such a requirement is not bad in itself; but it becomes bad if it worsens already declining standards of taste.

Technically, too, the special qualities of journalistic prose were in many ways beneficial. Writers could no longer afford to be longwinded or repetitive. The need was for economy and lightness of construction; and though verbal facility brings a lot of evils in its wake if abused it can, and in fact did, have a considerable influence for good stylistically. A lot of dead wood is pruned away on the sub-editor's table in any magazine or newspaper office.

Another and very important benefit was wrought by the new high-pressure journalism of the final decades of the nineteenth century: the almost insatiable demand for reading matter meant the establishment of many new journals. Inevitably, some of them, notably *The Atlantic, Harper's Magazine*, *Scribner's Monthly* and *The Yale Review* adopted critical standards from the outset; and for more than half a century they were to remain the forum of some of the most important writing of the western world.

CHAPTER FIVE

Later European Influences and the Conflict with Regionalism

I

WHITMAN spoke in the truly unique voice of an American writing about America for his fellow Americans; Melville spoke by implication of the unrest of a new and cosmopolitan nation discovering for itself the universal forces against which every member of that nation pitted his strength. Between them they raised American literature to a status comparable with that of Europe. But although America now had an authentic literary voice of its own, from which the rest of the world could deduce the American character and the American way of life, that voice still carried many overtures of Regionalism.

Regionalism is the cult of parochial dialect, humour and custom recorded by writers whose lesser genius usually excludes the ability to find a universal significance in the tales they tell. (Usually, but not always. Flaubert's *Madame Bovary* and William Faulkner's saga of Southern dissolution are examples of Regionalism in which that universal significance is attained.) None the less, the parochial associations of any literature are important because *in toto* they achieve by the pointilliste method a picture of a whole nation.

In a country so large as America isolation was an integral part of nineteenth century life. Distances between cities were so vast and travel so slow that there was no alternative to the self-contained community in which were developed small, almost independent, characteristic literatures that filled the gaps of time between arrivals from the nearest metropolis and the world beyond. The more rural the character of the community the greater was the need for a literary interpretation of its own folklore and people; and the regional schools of writing became most active during the period 1870–1900. The literature of those years records also the conflict between the new naturalistic approach of European models, already anticipated to a certain extent by Melville and Whitman, and the essential Romanticism by which the parochial writers in the main set store. This conflict was played out against the increasing tempo of industrialization and scientific progress; and the journalistic method was a weapon used by both parties in the conflict.

The short story and the essay were genres naturally suited to the newspaper and the periodical; and a recital of the names of the short-story writers who achieved an ephemeral fame during the period would fill several pages of this book. But such a recital is unnecessary. Fewer than half a dozen of them contributed anything to American literature that is seen in perspective to be important.

Of these, Francis Bret Harte specialized in tales of California, the mining region of the west. At the behest of the *Atlantic Monthly* and ten thousand dollars a year he specialized in them far too long and far too often, for he worked and reworked the same vein without ever developing its possibilities. But he had a nice sense of comic humour and a good ear for the grotesque speech of the west. He was himself an editor—of the *Overland Monthly* and *The Golden Era*—and possessed to the full the journalist's ability to sense a story of popular appeal.

Bret Harte was not an important writer in any sense of achievement or discovery—his observation is never more than skin deep, his feeling never more than sentimental—but he was able to hold a vast audience with tales that have remained collected and anthologized down to this day; and indeed among a handful of them—*The Luck of Roaring Camp, Miggles, The Outcasts of Poker Flat* and *The Idyll of Red Gulch*—there is every reason for retention, for his skill in simply holding the reader's attention from word to word is admirable.

> Mr. Oakhurst did not drink. It interfered with a profession which required coolness, impassiveness, and presence of mind, and, in his own language, he 'couldn't afford it.' As he gazed at his recumbent fellow-exiles, the loneliness begotten of his pariah-trade, his habits of life, his very vices, for the first time seriously oppressed him. He bestirred himself in dusting his black clothes, washing his hands and face, and other acts characteristic of his studiously neat habits, and for a moment forgot his annoyance. The thought of deserting his weaker and more pitiable companions never perhaps occurred to him. Yet he could not help feeling the want of that excitement which, singularly enough, was most conducive to that calm equanimity for which he was notorious. He looked at the gloomy walls that rose a thousand sheer feet above the circling pines around him; at the sky, ominously clouded; at the valley below, already deepening into shadow. And, doing so, he suddenly heard his own name called.

This paragraph from *The Outcasts of Poker Flat* shows that his style, though theatrical, is intensely readable; and easy readability, as has been mentioned, was an important factor in the rushing journalism of the day.

Bret Harte, though he was himself an Easterner by birth, established the journalistic convention of the Western mining town with its tough but sentimental characters, using the newspaperman's highlighting to obtain effects which amounted to hyperbole but which were justified in the cause of entertainment, since it was not the spirit of the Westerner that was being exploited but only his trappings and superficialities. Such justification cannot however be claimed for the writing of another regionalist who achieved immense popular appeal and whose influence has been unfortunately far reaching. This was Joel Chandler

Harris, whose Uncle Remus stories are well-known and well read even today, and whose tradition was followed by a score of magazine, film, stage and radio writers, all of whom, unintentionally but no less assuredly, have hindered the bridging of the gulf between black and white races.

Uncle Remus is the prototype of most of the vaudeville turns in which faces are blacked. He is the aged retainer of the once-rich families of the Southern States. He loves the children of these families with a devotion that is so dog-like as to be appallingly undignified in a human being; yet at the same time he is granted a spurious dignity of the dewy-eyed kind, a wisdom that comes from the ancient folklore of his race, and an implicit understanding that although he too is a creature of God, and as such is subject to conversion from his heathen ways, his mission in life is inevitably a servile one. He is often handsome; he often solves white people's problems in his own quaint way (and during these important times he is granted, as it were, a kind of sociological amnesty—a state in which a Virginia colonel or a Georgia grandmother may even touch him on the shoulder and be grateful with eyes filled with very white tears of inadequate gratitude); but he is never, in any circumstances, allowed to appear for any length of time as the mental or spiritual equal of the white-man-baas. The stories of Octavus Roy Cohen in the *Saturday Evening Post* today run as true to this formula as when Uncle Remus told his seven-year-old charge the story of *Brer Rabbit's Cradle* in 1880 in *The Atlanta Constitution*, the newspaper for which Joel Chandler Harris worked. Uncle Remus talks like this:

'I wish you'd tell me what you tote a hankcher for,' remarked Uncle Remus after he had reflected over the matter a little while.

'Why, to keep my mouth clean,' answered the little boy. Uncle Remus looked at the lad and shook his head doubtfully.

'Uh-uh!' he exclaimed. 'You can't fool folks when dey git ez old ez what I is. I been watching you now more days dan I kin count, an' I aint never seen yo' mouf dirty 'nuff fer ter be wiped wid a hankcher. It's allers clean—too clean fer ter suit me. Dar's yo' pa, now; when he wuz a little chap like you, his mouf useter git dirty in de mornin' an' stay dirty plum twell night. Dey wa'n't scarcely a day dat he didn't look like he been playin' wid de pigs in de stable lot. Ef he yever is tote a hankcher, he ain't never show it ter me.'

There is a basic truth at the heart of the exaggerated dialect, just as there is basic truth in the assumption of writers of the *Mrs. Wiggs* school that all cockneys say 'ain't' and 'naou' and 'wot.' The dialect doesn't much matter, a convention has made it acceptable.

What does matter is that the Negro had the Uncle Remus pattern forced upon him by people who unjustifiably assumed that with their class privilege and the colour of their flesh went the right to create a convention that future Negroes must adhere to and future whites be born into believing. And in the case of Joel Chandler Harris's writings this was being done less than twenty years after a whole bloody war had been fought for Negro emancipation. The emancipation had been won, but it had been merely physical; the negro remained spiritually in bondage and it was easier to perpetuate that bondage by the word than by the fetter.

Harris, then, established a convention about the Negro race—a convention that was not to be argued until the race itself became creatively literate to the extent of being able to form a branch of literature that was genuinely Negro. That branch shall be discussed in its proper place.

George W. Cable, a New Orleans warehouse clerk, was a regionalist writer of much the same calibre as Bret Harte and Harris; but his principal theme was the legendary past of his native city. He did not, even obliquely, imply feelings of racial discrimination. There is not much to be usefully said about him except that he portrayed the South as Harte had portrayed the West and that he helped preserve a little longer the romantic traditions against the incoming pressure of European naturalism. For all his stories are enshrouded in the mists of nostalgia through which one can faintly discern the figures of feudal grandeur dancing in the ballrooms of the past to the sound of music echoing through the halls of looking-glass:

> The sun broke through a clearing sky, and Babtiste pronounced it good for luck. There had been a hurricane in the night. The weed-grown tile roofs were still dripping and from lofty brick and low adobe walls a rising steam responded to the summer sunlight. Upstreet, and across the Rue du Canal, one could get glimpses of the Gardens in Faubourg Ste. Marie standing in silent wretchedness, so many tearful Lucretias, tattered victims of the storm. Short remnants of the wind now and then came down the narrow street in erratic puffs heavily laden with odours of broken boughs and torn flowers, skimmed the little pools of rain-water in the deep ruts of the unpaved streets, and suddenly went away to nothing, like a juggler's butterflies.

And as spokesman for the East there was a writer who was in some ways the finest regionalist of all, Sarah Orne Jewett.

The daughter of a doctor who lived in South Berwick, Maine, she went with her father on all his rounds and developed a missionary zeal to present the New Englanders in their proper simplicity and with their surrounding countryside falling into a rather terrible, if slow, decay. This disintegration was in its way strangely idyllic, it was a disintegration of the most terrible kind because the most natural—the disintegration of old age; and Sarah Orne Jewett handled her Indian-summer themes with infinite tenderness that never drifted into sentimentality.

Although remarkable among the regionalists for the quality of her local colour she is important in another way. She was in too close touch with realism ever to be designated a romantic, in spite of the decaying romance that motivates her work; and she must therefore be given a position where she can be seen in perspective to have used the methods of both schools and to have acted as an important link between them. If one is to consider any kind of transitional bridge between romanticism and naturalism, then it is in the work of Sarah Orne Jewett that one can most easily see evidence of the change.

It would be quite just to point to the eclectic quality of Miss Jewett's work. She had read and admired the stories of that other writer whose people moved in the environment of New England, Harriet Beecher Stowe. But although Mrs Stowe had achieved a great success with *Uncle Tom's Cabin* ten years before the Civil War, and had presented the abstract problem of slavery in a way that compelled her reader's attention, she had turned aside from the sociological theme and concentrated on local-colour stories of her native New England that were nothing like so compelling as *Uncle Tom's Cabin*, ill-constructed and melodramatic though that book was. So it must be to Miss Jewett's *The Country of the Pointed Firs* rather than Mrs Stowe's *Old Town Folks* that we must look for the best-drawn picture of the Maine seaboard. The South Berwick doctor's daughter was by far the better technician, and she had a sensitivity much finer than the older woman's.

II

The regional, colloquial writing of the post-Civil War period naturally helped to broaden the frontiers of literature. Metropolitan readers were responding with ready pleasure to the bucolic goings-on of their distant kinsmen, who in turn were learning more and more of the life of the big cities. All this was being accomplished by the rushing presses of periodical and daily journalism.

Everywhere there was a genuine interest, a desire to know how the other man lived, that was continually being fostered by the great name and the great works of Whitman. Regionalism also served in a way as a bulwark against the incoming flood of naturalism. It was the final stand of the Romantics, and it failed only because local colour, quaint dialect, odd customs—all the trappings of atmosphere—are not in themselves the heart of a literature. Something bigger is needed: the interpretation of human experience on a scale that is independent of any restrictions imposed by *locale*. Such an interpretation was now the prerogative of European writers, and was to remain so until their influence had permeated more fully into American literature. Melville, though he lived till 1891, had been too great for the times and the literature that he flooded with his mighty spirit, and he remained virtually unsung until his centenary in 1919. Only Whitman had been able to pitch his voice in a key acceptable to the multitudes and at the same time demonstrate that his stature was that of a unique genius. In any case, as has been shown, both Whitman and Melville had germinated the seeds of naturalism in their works; and Sarah Orne Jewett, though by no means a genius, had furthered their growth. All three writers, then, had established a kind of literary fifth column within the very bulwark of Romanticism that was the mainstay of their work. Because of this internal weakening American literature was flowing more easily into its new course, aided by the influx of another set of influences from Europe.

III

There is a distinction in literary theory between naturalism and realism. Briefly, realism is the literary movement concerned with interpreting life as realistically as possible within the bounds of creative imagination.

Realism will have nothing to do with the beautifying of people or attitudes for the sake of effect; none the less it requires that the novelist shall select for his story only those incidents which shall be susceptible of moulding into an aesthetically satisfactory shape. Naturalism, on the other hand, is less concerned with aesthetically satisfactory shapes than with ensuring that only the moral values of materialism are sustained. It operates specifically in the sphere of social environment and seeks to show that life is tragic because of the defections of human nature at the present stage of man's evolution.

In practice, naturalism and realism often intermingle, the antithesis of romanticism being their common denominator, and here they will be considered together as a single movement. One can easily become confused in trying to trace the origins of any 'ism' and in any case it is a profitless task, for even if such an origin could be determined it would not be of shattering importance. But the curious can find strong naturalistic tendencies in the sociological lyrics of Thomas Hood (e.g. *The Song of the Shirt*) and in the novels of Victor Hugo (*Les Miserables*); and in the work of the collaborating Goncourt brothers there is much stronger evidence.

The curiously intimate creative liaison between these two brothers resulted in *Germinie Lacerteux* and *Manette Saloman*, both intensely realistic studies of nemesis set against an extremely morbid background. Germinie Lacerteux is a nymphomaniac servant girl who is seduced by a villain who deserts her, thus ensuring her complete degradation. The authors bestow on their tragic heroine a certain compassion, which increases the stature of the novel; but the theme is used by a later naturalistic writer, the Irishman George Moore, in *Esther Waters*, to much better effect, and it is through George Moore that the Goncourts have effected their influence, rather than directly.

Emile Zola, on the other hand, had a very direct influence (though his works were necessarily read furtively and usually in dubious translations); for it was quickly discerned that the journalist who was forced to leave France after his championship of Captain Dreyfus in the famous 'J'accuse' article in the newspaper *Aurore* was also a novelist with a huge corpus of work to his credit.

And strange and shocking work it was. It aroused immense hostility in his native France and its printing in England was the cause of his publisher's imprisonment. (In passing it is salutary to note that a highly reputable English publisher, wishing to produce *La Terre* for the first time in England in 1954, sought a printer for many months before one who was willing to print the book was discovered.) From *Therese Raquin* in 1867, through all the twenty volumes of *Les Rougon-Macquart* to the agrarian crudities of *La Terre* in 1887, Zola's countrymen never ceased to shudder at the realism they could not quite face; while the countrymen of other lands induced vicarious enjoyment by reading goggle-eyed the infelicitous translations that were seeping across from France.

To Zola, and particularly to *Le Ventre de Paris*, a novel set in the huge public market Les Halles, may be traced the technique of the newspaper reporter expanded and elaborated until it becomes a record of the observations of a creative artist rather than the method of a mere reporter who is interested only in a photographic description in words; for every minute detail is carefully collected and assembled in the way that will allow it its maximum effect. And it is this technical method that all naturalistic writers have in common—a method that has since become so common in American literature as to be unremarkable, but which at the end of the nineteenth century proved to be the death, or at any rate the burial alive, of the Romantic movement. For Zola was the first writer since Rabelais to use the undiluted (but nevertheless carefully selected) language of the gutter; and everyone with any knowledge at all of American literature today knows just how popular that characteristic of naturalism has become.

There were other French naturalistic writers whose influence has in the main been less because of translation difficulties or because their work has a less immediate appeal.

Flaubert's *Madame Bovary*, for example, one of the masterpieces of fiction of all time, belongs to the genre of naturalism but is more or less untranslatable; for Flaubert was a perfectionist who would sweat for a fortnight over a single sentence, and the French language is the most precise in the world. The theme of *Bovary*, however, has exerted its own special influence, and the crop of fading carbon copies of bourgeois pettiness as exemplified in Flaubert's heroine never seems to diminish either in England or America.

Guy de Maupassant and Ernest Hemingway can be seen in line by most people. But Maupassant, perfectionist of the short story, once remarked, 'The mediocrity of the universe astonishes and disgusts me, the littleness of everything nauseates me, and the poverty of human beings crushes me,' and there is indeed an essential misanthropy that motivates his work—a misanthropy quite foreign to Hemingway, who wrote one of the most sincerely compassionate stories of all time, *The Light of the World*, and whose roots will be seen, when the time comes to examine them, to be firmly bedded in the soil of Romanticism. No: Maupassant's influence has been mainly through the technique of the form of the short story, which has been carefully studied by such writers as Somerset Maugham, rather than through the innate cynicism that was conveyed with much better effect by Zola.

Thomas Hardy's great tragedies have exerted an influence on American naturalistic writing largely through an error in American comprehension. For Hardy was in fact a fatalistic—in the Sophoclean and Æschylean sense—rather than a naturalistic writer. In fact when all the tragedies of *Jude the Obscure* have been brought to their fatal ends Jude Fawley exclaims in the actual words of the Agamemnon chorus: 'Nothing can be done. Things are as they are, and will be brought to their destined issue.'

Hardy's books were naturally more accessible to English-speaking audiences, and *Jude the Obscure* had the additional advantage of a public outcry against its exploitation of the impulses of sex to aid its influence. But it is the fact that he always chose themes of unrelieved tragedy, rather than his philosophy, that has impressed Hardy's mark on American literature.

George Moore, on the other hand, had a fairly direct naturalistic influence, particularly through his two finest works, *Confessions of a Young Man* and *Esther Waters*.

Moore was an Irishman who lived in Paris for ten years and absorbed many of that city's artistic influences before moving to London and beginning a career as a novelist. The *Confessions*, which told of Moore's early years in Paris, were extremely popular in America, and when *Esther Waters* was published six years later its public was already prepared.

Esther Waters, as has already been said, derives from the Goncourt brothers' *Germinie Lacerteux*, but it has far more conviction than the French book. Esther is a servant girl who is seduced and deserted, driven from shelter and eventually offered a good marriage which she refuses in order that she may capitulate to the bestial charms of her original lover and ultimately find herself back—still a servant—in the house of her downfall. Without bitterness, Moore has recounted the number and variety of ways in which a servant girl can be victimized in the Victorian era; and he has shown as the subject of his study a human being of stature who, knowing that all the odds of social environment are against her, uses the richness of experience to build her own character.

Stylistically, the book is atrocious. Oscar Wilde remarked that Moore had to write for seven years before he knew there was such a thing as grammar and for another seven before he realized a paragraph had structure; and although toward the end of his life Moore was paradoxically enchanted by the works of that super-stylist Walter Pater, he never succeeded in achieving a semblance of style for himself. *Esther Waters*, his finest novel, is full of bits like this:

> On week days he wore a short jacket, and every day a ring of discoloured hair, neither brown nor red, but the neutral tint that hair which does not turn grey acquires under his chin.

It is unfortunate that the infelicities of the style, as well as the good construction and masterly characterization have also had their influence on American (and English) writing.

In summary, then: Zola, the Goncourts and George Moore are the main sources of European naturalistic influence, with Flaubert, Hardy and Maupassant bearing off as less influential tributaries.

IV

Stephen Crane is often referred to as 'the father' of American naturalism. That such a parentage is dubious will be seen when the time comes to discuss his work.

If one is to accept the usual definition of naturalism, i.e. that it is the philosophy that shows man as a creature whose fate is shaped by circumstances beyond his control, then there are definite indications of that philosophy as early as the work of Melville—and certainly in Whitman. There are even stronger indications in the short stories of Hamlin Garland and the novels of William Dean Howells—both of whom preceded Crane in the field of naturalism—though admittedly not by many years.

Howells was a cosmopolitan journalist who was rewarded for a biography of Abraham Lincoln by being appointed to the American consulate in Venice. There he absorbed the European mode of mannered living with epicurean sensitivity and returned to America to take up an appointment with the *Nation* and subsequently the editorship of the *Atlantic Monthly*. The *milieu* in which Howells works most successfully is the comedy of manners, and here Jane Austen has clearly been his mentor in wit; but all his comedies of manners incorporate some appreciation of the realistic side of life. In the best one, *The Rise of Silas Lapham*, Howells presents the problem of the business tycoon who loses everything, including his wife's trust, because he is unable to cope with the life of big business that has come his way by chance (or fate) and who can only draw blindly on his natural honesty for a solution to his problems. There is an irony in Howells' recognition of Lapham as typical of the individualistic upholder of private enterprise who is faced with the temptation of improving his own lot by giving way to the corruption of corporate enterprise. It is in his recognition of the encroaching blandishments of corruption that Howells is most successful in motivating the tenets of realism.

As a literary critic Howells had considerable influence, and since he was never confused by any doubt as to the necessity of the novelist's exploitation of realism he was able to recognize the truth at the heart of the work of a Middle Westerner, Hamlin Garland.

Garland's best work is contained in two volumes of short stories, *Main-Travelled Roads* and *Prairie Folks*. Here is to be found no single concession to refinement or romanticism. There are some impressionistic touches, as when he writes of 'the wild geese, honking wildly, as they sprawled sidewise down the wind,' but the themes are without exception sombre (though not without touches of native humour) and the style in the main correspondingly Spartan:

> She rose from the cow's side at last, and taking her pails of foaming milk, staggered toward the gate. The two pails hung from her lean arms, her bare feet slipped on the filthy ground, her greasy and faded calico dress showed her tired and swollen ankles.

and again from the same story:

> The man thrust his dirty, naked feet into his huge boots, and, without washing his face or combing his hair, went out to the barn.

There is nothing particularly revolting to the modern reader in such snapshots, and in fact there is nothing particularly revolting in the people observed: such living is more or less normal on many farms even in England today (for it would be idle to pretend that a farm labourer would find it natural or logical to shave and preen himself before milking cows at dawn on a winter's morning); but what was shocking at the end of the nineteenth century was the deliberate casting aside of euphemism or turn of phrase that might at least have made the squalor more acceptable. Garland had a passion for social justice (which motivates all his work) and no less a passion for recording the seamy side as he saw it; and it must be remembered that Romanticism was still secure in position if deficient in magnitude. Here were some of the early infiltrations of European naturalistic influence and people were not ready to accept them presented as crudely as this; they therefore turned aside from Garland's fiction and did not turn to him again until the literary climate had completely changed and naturalism was an accepted thing; then, in 1917, his autobiography, *A Son of the Middle Border*, became a best seller and a classic of American rural life.

The public that was still avidly reading Scott and *Ben Hur* was even less ready to accept the early work of Stephen Crane—particularly when they knew of his Bohemian existence and his methods of attracting notoriety. But Crane's life was tragically short—he was only twenty-nine when he died cf tuberculosis—and it is only in perspective that he is seen to be of immense importance in the school of naturalistic writing, though not actually an instigator of the method.

Crane's first book, a *conte* called *Maggie*, is clearly an imitation of Zola's *L'Assommoir*. This story of a slum girl whose potential purity is ravished by a bartender, a drunken mother and a violent brother, and who ends a subsequent career of prostitution by drowning herself, was rejected even by the magazine that published Hamlin Garland's work and had to be privately printed and financed by borrowed money until after Crane's success with his most famous book, *The Red Badge of Courage*. It is fair to add that the hostility with which the book was received was in the main due to Crane's failure to tell his story from any particular moral viewpoint. There is not even the positive strength of misanthropy to back the story up; and *Maggie* is now chiefly interesting for its faithful recording—for the first time and with great success—of strong dialogue. Crane's journalistically trained ear was always to serve him in good stead in the matter of dialogue and impressionistic sentences.

The Red Badge of Courage was published in the Philadelphia *Free Press* as a serial—Hamlin Garland having paid for the typing of it as a gesture of faith in his young friend's abilities. Book publication followed in New York and London—where Crane was compared (with extraordinary ineptness) to Kipling, greeted as a brilliant new writer and accepted immediately into the literary circle of Henry James and Joseph Conrad.

The Red Badge is far from original as regards the elements of its story: Zola's *La Debâcle*, Tolstoy's *Sevastapol*, Ambrose Bierce's *One Officer, One Man*, a series of articles called *Recollections of a Private* by Warren Lee Goss—these have all contributed in one way or another to the story of the Civil War which for the first time in American fiction did nothing whatever to glamorize battle and everything to realize the truth about it. But it is none the less a good story of a single great battle seen through the consciousness of a single combatant, Henry Fleming, who is hit on the head with a gun by a comrade even more terrified than he is when both of them are running away in understandable terror, and who subsequently is taken for a hero and finds it perfectly easy to act like one.

Bravery had not been treated so cynically before and the public cared little that Crane had never in his life seen a battle himself; he was picturing for them the emotions felt by the ordinary ranker—the weariness, the cold, the complete lack of knowledge of what the battle was about and whether it had been won or lost. It was all fresh and had nothing whatever to do with the heroics of war they had seen pictured in a thousand sentimental engravings of the *Soldier's Farewell to His Horse* variety and read of in the melodramatic dispatches of the Romanticists. War had long been democratic in theory; now its actual physical emotions were set before the common soldier on his own level and he was able to dispense with the feeling of shame which he had imagined, in the face of denial by glamour, to be exclusively his own.

As for Crane's literary style, it is curiously uneven. Fresh and natural images like 'the crimson terror of an exploding shell, with fibres of flame that seemed like lances' jostle against bits of obfuse overwriting of this kind:

> When he knew that he and his comrades had failed to do anything in successful ways and that might bring the little pangs of a kind of remorse upon the officer, the youth allowed the rage of the baffled to possess him. This cold officer upon a monument, who dropped epithets unconcernedly down, would be finer as a dead man, he thought. So grievous did he think it that he could never possess the secret right to taunt truly in answer.

But the important thing about Crane is not his literary style but the fact that he applied naturalistic innovations to a theme, war, that had hitherto been treated as sacredly heroic; and it is in his work that one can find the roots of practically all the naturalistic war stories of the twentieth century—not only *The Naked and the Dead* but *All Quiet on the Western Front* too.

V

Naturalism gained two more fairly important exponents in America before it reached its apotheosis in the work of Theodore Dreiser—'the Hindenburg of the novel' as the critic H. L. Mencken called him. These were Frank Norris and Jack London.

Norris's naturalistic influence was weakened by an early addiction to the romances of Robert Louis Stevenson; and it is doubtful whether, in spite of his later stern devotion to Zola, he ever really believed in the earthy saga *Wheat*, which he planned as a trilogy but of which he lived only long enough to complete two volumes—*The Octopus* and *The Pit*; for in both these books and in

McTeague, Norris's other big novel, there is a latent romanticism that takes the regrettable form of Nietschean super heroes of the blond-beast type. At heart Norris was really a romantic who saw the cogency of the argument of naturalism and supported it against his inmost feelings.

Jack London had a much more durable success than Norris. This was largely because in the materialistic and increasingly socialistic world that ushered in the twentieth century, London couched his materialism always in terms of violent action, and always in terms derogatory to the middle classes from which he himself came. He too had a secret love of red-blooded romanticism and may be likened to the shrewd self-made Englishman who uses brain instead of brawn and whose motto is 'Don't fight—fiddle.'

London led the adventurous life of the man who goes to find out for himself. He had been a deckhand, tramp (with prison sentences for vagrancy), university student, newsboy, ruffian, Klondike gold prospector and countless other things. But since childhood he had the all-consuming desire to become an author, and on his unsuccessful return from the Klondike he set himself the task of writing a book on Alaskan adventure stories, *The Son of the Wolf*.

No particular success attended his new venture, but London was scarcely the type of man to be put off. He tried again, this time with a novel, *The Call of the Wild*, and there success surely was; for the regionalism of Bret Harte (however lusty) and Sarah Orne Jewett (however perceptive) stood little chance in a conflict with the universal primitive emotion of exultation that inspired the pages of this tale of the struggle for existence in the frozen wastes.

The story of the dog Buck, who is taken from the effete atmosphere of his Californian home and set down in the Arctic is really an interpretation of the Nietschean philosophy of mastery by superior intelligence; it is also symbolic of London's lifelong chip-on-the-shoulder attitude toward class distinctions and the force that inspired his firm belief in social evolution and the Marxian doctrine of the ultimate triumph of the proletariat.

London subsequently became an agitator and was as boring as most dogmatic preachers in his platform lectures and books like *The War of the Classes*. He could never quite forget that he was an illegitimate child and that until *The Call of the Wild* was published he had been rejected by every magazine and publisher in the United States. His importance lies not in his literary style—though at its best it is a sound, vivid style—but in the fact that he administered a salutary knock to what he thought of as the 'literary notion' that man's existence needs only a spiritual interpretation. Since *The Call of the Wild* there has arisen a whole school of atavistic, 'red-blooded' fiction that has taken good care to ensure that the place of adventure on the physical level has not been forgotten. In fact this school ensures, in countless paper-backs and magazine stories, that it is only too well remembered.

CHAPTER SIX

Reformers and Reactionaries

I

THE turn of the century saw the United States' attainment of authoritative status among the world powers. Her economy was disrupted by the depression of 1893, by crop failures and labour troubles and by international disputes—especially the Spanish-American war of 1898; but from all these adversities she emerged victorious and with immense prestige. And to prove to the world that her achievements were not only materialistic America had exhibited a determination to spread culture by any and every means. This meant in effect that education was compulsory in nearly all states and territories and that the big cities supported symphony orchestras, opera, and museums and art galleries. Such a culture was of course artificial in the sense that it was imposed from without rather than having its source in the necessity of expression; and it is to be noted that this cultural veneer has remained a characteristic of the American people. The literary evidence can be seen, for example, in the many commercially successful book clubs that specialize in dispensing copies of the classics in 'exquisite' bindings (particularly those classics, e.g. Boccaccio and Apuleius, that offer the vicarious enjoyment of unproscribable 'obscenity'); in the libraries of unopened volumes belonging to tycoons and commuters alike; and in the lip service paid to literature by the film, radio and television industries. It can also be seen in the determined overt lusts of the average contemporary American; but this is a subject for the anthropologist rather than the literary surveyor. The point of interest to the present reader is, that with the rise of America to world-power status and the enormous materialistic success of the monopolization of industry by private enterprise, there has been a corresponding increase in the self-consciousness of American culture—not the simple self-consciousness that recognizes the necessity of technical skill in any branch of art, but the more ominous self-consciousness that recognizes that culture is a necessary thing, that it is the 'done' thing to have home-made schools of literature, painting and music. It is also noteworthy that since that rise to power there has been a levelling out, if not an actual decline, in the attainments of American literature. In fact only one writer, William Faulkner, seems to have attained a stature that in the general perspective appears comparable to that of Melville or Whitman. But it is equally noteworthy that writers of that stature do not occur frequently in the literature of any country.

The identification of the historic background is of only the slightest importance—as certain trees and buildings may be important as identity marks in a landscape. It must be remembered that literature, if it is to be of the utmost value, must be prophetic in the sense that it should enable us to anticipate the events of history. Of course we are never sensible enough to anticipate anything; but that is hardly the fault of literature, which at its highest level goes on holding up the mirror, as Stendhal put it, along the road of life, but always holding it so that there is a glimpse of the traffic coming the other way round the next corner.

It will be clear by now that the preoccupation with material things that formed the basis of the American way of life at the beginning of the twentieth century had been appreciated by those writers who had established the naturalistic movement in literature. Equally, it had been appreciated by the Romanticists, who offered their own idealized views of humanity and living and in doing so turned themselves into reactionaries in conflict with the reformers.

Although Romanticism has never faded from ken, except as a literary theory, it is true to say that its survival has depended to a large extent on its sentimental aspect, which in time, as will be seen, spread to the reformers' camp and became an inverted realism, exemplified in the work, for example, of Ernest Hemingway. But at the end of the nineteenth century it was under the sentence of banishment formulated in the critical edict of W. D. Howells in *Criticism and Fiction*:

> 1. Minimize plot, avoiding the complex, unnatural manipulation which makes the author master of a puppet show.
> 2. Avoid romantic distortion and aristocratic setting.
> 3. Subscribe not to the hero cult, for it is a feudalistic survival.
> 4. Glorify the ordinary, even when discovering it in all its straw-hatted familiarity.

The reasonably critical reader may feel that however else American literature has failed, it has succeeded only too well in glorifying the ordinary.

II

The naturalism which had been merely hinted at in the delicate observation of Sarah Orne Jewett in the eighteen-eighties reached a full and sombre cadence in the work of Theodore Dreiser, whose first novel, *Sister Carrie*, was published in 1900. Historic events, the changing scene, industrialization and the vast increase in population had all combined in establishing the materialistic outlook; and the European literary influences of Zola, Chateaubriand and the rest had been opportunely to hand to interpret it and keep always at least one step ahead of actual development—seldom more because of the breathless speed at which things were happening.

Dreiser's early life was one of poverty and depression; but that can scarcely have been the cause of his utter nihilism. Many finer writers than Dreiser have washed dishes, driven wagons, stolen money, worked on pulp magazines and gutter newspapers and achieved a gay and positive philosophy from it all. The cause of Dreiser's negation of life, which he expressed himself:

> I cannot imagine any explanation or interpretation of any life, my own included, that would be either true—or important, if true. Life is to me too much of a welter and play of inscrutable forces to permit, in my case at least, any significant comment. One may paint for one's own entertainment, and that of others—perhaps. As I see him, the utterly infinitesimal individual weaves among the mysteries a floss-like and wholly meaningless course—if course it be. In short, I catch no meaning from all I have seen, and pass quite as I came, confused and dismayed

is, paradoxically in a writer, caused by too much reading with a mind that was limited in its scope. Like George Gissing, he thought that education for life in Grub Street was education for life in the world; but Dreiser never even discovered the truth that Gissing ultimately clung to, that 'the only thing known to us of absolute value is artistic perfection.' He speaks of himself as one of the people

> who cannot make up their minds about anything. I read and read. . . . But I find that one history contradicts another. . . . And I sit here and read . . . wondering

and he never in his finest moments achieves the prose style of which Gissing was capable. In fact he never achieves a style at all. And his mind remained to the end the mind of a nonentity—provincial, unstable, Teutonic and dull. Only at the end of his life (he died in 1945) did he forget to deceive even himself and spit on Naturalism in an anti-war pamphlet, *America Is Worth Saving*. Too late one perceives that the man was a sentimentalist at heart and would have made a very good one if he could have borne to admit it even to himself.

However, his achievement in Naturalism is a considerable one because of its far-reaching influence and its massive proportions. When he has little to say he impresses, like the Biggest Aspidistra in the World, by size alone; and in the number of words he writes in only five novels, and in the diversity of characters, each one of them observed in a multiplicity of detail, he does indeed exert the hypnotism of hugeness.

Sister Carrie, his first novel, and *Jennie Gerhardt*, his second, are both derived from the *Esther Waters* story of George Moore; but Dreiser denies his Carrie and his Jennie the intelligence Moore gave to Esther, and he likewise denies them the compassion he gave the villains of a later book, *The Financier*.

The Financier is in fact one of the best books about monopolistic enterprise in American literature—so long as one is content to absorb the theme without coming across the slightest hint of irony, of which Dreiser is quite incapable. *The Titan*, which followed it, is as minuscule in its content as it is titanic in name and shape. It adds nothing whatever to the earlier story, of which it was intended to be a continuation, and the nihilistic message of the two books can be adequately grasped from a single passage in the former:

> The damnable scheme of things which we call existence brings about conditions whereby whole masses suffer who have no cause to suffer, and, on the other hand, whole masses joy who have no cause to joy. It rains on the just and the unjust impartially. We suffer for our temperaments, which we did not make, and our weaknesses and lacks, which are no part of our willing or doing. Who by taking thought can add one cubit to his stature? Who can make his brain better? His thoughts

> swifter? His courage greater? Who is it that can do anything it was not given him to do? All good things are gifts. There are no creations of the mind alone. Creations, achievements, distinguished results always sink back into so many other things. They have their roots in inherited ability, in environment, in fortune, in a lucky star. There is no possible contradiction in this. So it was ever. So it will be from everlasting to everlasting.

The Genius, Dreiser's fourth novel, is about a painter who thinks, dreams and lives sex and pornography. It is a 750-page bore.

Dreiser's last and greatest novel was published in 1925. It is called *An American Tragedy* and the title is not inept, for in this story of Clyde Griffiths, a boy who is trapped by the conflict between desire and environment, Dreiser has indeed found the cathartic secret of absolute tragedy, and the reader is caught in an austerely magnificent sweep of emotions that is morally elevating in spite of the gloom of the story. What Dreiser really achieved for Naturalism in *An American Tragedy* was the proof that insignificant man, as well as heroic man (as in the Theban plays, or in *Lear* or *Hamlet*), is susceptible to suffering and responding —not with the eloquent heroism of Œdipus (who at least believes in the Fate that has caused his downfall) but with the uncomprehending heroism of acceptance that is never surrender. Something of the human spirit shines here in spite of Dreiser's insistent negation; and its brightness is brighter because of the dullness that surrounds it.

No writer could have been less sophisticated in his realization of the potentialities of technique than the blundering Dreiser: none could have been more sensible of the elegances of style than Henry James. Yet both were adherents of the naturalistic school. But while Dreiser achieved his results by the hit-and-miss method of the sculptor who simply lacks the vision to imagine the completed statue he has been commissioned to do and goes on adding lumps of clay until the head he intended has turned into an equestrian figure ninety feet high, James is concerned solely with the epicurean concept of art he learnt from the Russian Turgenev.

James, though a New Yorker by birth, lived in Europe from 1875 until his death in 1916, and his work, though immensely influential directly or indirectly on many of the writers of Europe and America who followed him, cannot justly be said to have added anything to American literature by its possession of any national characteristics. From first to last James was a citizen of the world, preoccupied with technique and the refinements of style; and although several of his novels introduce American characters the introduction is usually effected to bring out the contrast between the ingenuous American and the sophisticated European.

One of the writers through whom Henry James exerted much influence on American literature was Edith Wharton, a woman of patrician birth and aristocratic breeding, whose *milieu* is the fashionable and cosmopolitan New York of the end of the nineteenth century. Mrs Wharton's work will be considered in a later chapter where it more naturally belongs, as will the work of another regionalist, Willa Cather. For the moment it is more relevant to consider the development of another aspect of American literature, an aspect which—alas!—can conveniently be referred to only by the upstage label of Freudian.

III

The Gothic horrors of Poe had their origin in a psychological state for which there was at that time no common name. It was the investigations of Sigmund Freud that made the noun 'complex' popular in the language and stimulated an interest in the relationship between psychopathic diseases and repressed sexual desires. Largely because of ridicule and prudish resentment it took some time for the discoveries of Freud to permeate into the public conscience. But this was hardly the fault of American fiction, which lost no time at all in exploring the possibilities of what probably appeared a new field of human interest.

Of course it wasn't new at all; but the fact that now the human mind could be explained in terms that had the closest relationship to both story telling and creative ability was of paramount importance. One could now self-consciously explore the mind and its motivations and set down one's findings in terms that the reader could readily understand. The Œdipus complex, the inferiority complex, the father fixation—these began to be common coinage as soon as fiction writers used them; and for a long time the 'psychological' novel held sway. In fact it is only recently that people have begun to realize that all novels are psychological because all lives are psychological.

Gertrude Stein, a Jewess born in Allegheny, Pennsylvania, in 1874, made a name for herself by going to Paris after studying psychology under William James (brother of Henry) at Harvard and trying to transfer the abstractions of the cubists Bracque and Picasso into literary terms. The 'psychology' of her experiment, she claimed, lay in the fact that it was all carried out under the spell of automatic writing and that she had eliminated all narrative in her verses: she just sought the individual value of words and deliberately eschewed any kind of external associations:

> 'Arthur two our age change will tree behaviour for finally left come to such now their stability compress in union against made hence for the close of establishment leak and forfeit a plenty of united practice of their popularity just now goes as made a piece of inclined to their fairly . . .'

With the aid of elaborate publicity Gertrude Stein convinced a number of people whose receptiveness was tempered by the prevailing craziness of the pre-war years that there was an exquisite sense in her esoteric nonsense.

But although there is no doubt of the practical worthlessness of 'poems' of this kind there is equally no doubt that what Gertrude Stein was trying to do was important. For her purpose from the beginning had been to demonstrate Freud's theory that beneath the ordinary consciousness of the human mind there lay another, and vastly more important, stratum—the subconscious. She realized that if the conscious and the subconscious minds could be shown as capable of operating independently it would be the subconscious that would be seen to represent the primeval impulses of human action. Hence the attempt at setting down the words uttered by the subconscious when under the spell of the mild hypnosis that induced automatic writing.

It was of course an impossible task she had set herself, for the subconscious utterances of one person are unintelligible alike to that same person's conscious apprehension and the apprehension of others. But it proved later to be an important hare she had loosed; for later writers (notably Dorothy M. Richardson in England and James Joyce in Ireland) showed that if the creative imagination is allowed to explore the subconscious there is practically no limit to the effects that can be achieved. Thus the stream-of-consciousness narrative and the interior monologue came into being.

Gertrude Stein wrote one important book of fiction before returning to her preoccupation with the notion of an abstract literature: this was the trilogy of *contes*, *Three Lives*, containing the all-important story *Melanctha*.

Melanctha is a study of the primitive emotions of a 'pale yellow and mysterious' negro girl Melenctha Herbert, her friend Rose Johnson and her lovers Jem Richards and Jeff Campbell. Its purpose is not so much to show the conflicting emotions of the quartet as to prove the importance of the time element in the matching of passions. But its importance in the perspective of American literature lies in the fact of its being the first genuine study of primitives *in the primitive manner*, just as Picasso's 1907 abstractions were the first simplified interpretations of the already simplified negro carvings; and its influence can be followed with ease through the 'lost generation' of writers (it was Gertrude Stein's own phrase) right down to the present day and the primitivistic plays and stories of Tennessee Williams.

But it was necessarily a small public to whom Gertrude Stein appealed. Even in the days of her greatest fame her publishers printed only two thousand copies of each of her books. As with Henry James, hers was an influence that was to be disseminated slowly—and in the main indirectly.

One of the first writers to be affected by her was Sherwood Anderson, who returned from the Spanish-American war to his small home town in Ohio and settled down as the manager of a paint factory—to live respectably, one would have thought, for the rest of his natural life. But Anderson tells in his autobiography, *Story Teller's Story*, how one day he was dictating a letter to his secretary when he stopped in the middle of a sentence and told her:

> My dear young woman; it is all very silly but I have decided to no longer concern myself with this buying and selling. It may be all right for others but for me it is poison. There is the factory. You may have it if it pleases you. It is of little value I dare say. Now at this moment, with the letter I have been dictating, with the very sentence you have been writing left unfinished, I am going out that door and never coming back. What am I to do? Well, now, that I don't know. I am going to wander about. I am going to sit with people, listen to words, tell tales of people, what they are thinking what they are feeling.

And tell tales Anderson did—most of the early ones influenced by Dreiser, rather clumsy and sentimental.

Then in 1919 came the book of short stories with which he gained favour, *Winesburg, Ohio*.

In their choice of themes the *Winesburg* stories show a changed influence—this time of Gertrude Stein. Most of them are plotless sketches with the primeval instincts of brutal men to motivate them. In most of them there is an innocent and bewildered victim who is studied sympathetically, and often sentimentally. *Hands* is typical: it tells of a sensitive and introspective schoolmaster whose affectionate hands are the delight of a half-witted schoolboy who dreams 'unspeakable things and in the morning went forth to tell his dreams as facts.'

> Adolphe Meyers was driven from the Pennsylvanian town in the night. With lanterns in their hands a dozen men came to the door of the house where he lived alone and commanded that he dress and come forth. It was raining and one of the men had a rope in his hands. They had intended to hang the schoolmaster, but something in his figure, so small, white, and pitiful, touched their hearts and they let him escape. As he ran away into the darkness they repented of their weakness and ran after him, swearing and throwing sticks and great balls of mud at the figure that screamed and ran faster and faster into the darkness.

The self-conscious simplicity of the style is perhaps more the imitation of the Old Testament than of Gertrude Stein; and there are many tricks of biblical style that Anderson retains throughout his work—notably the frequent use of the conjunction 'and' to begin a paragraph (a trick that is useful in stimulating the effect of action where none actually exists) and the deliberately short sentences; but the interest in psychology and the attempts to display the psychological motives of characters is derived entirely from Gertrude Stein. Anderson's later volumes of stories, *The Triumph of the Egg* and *Death in the Woods*, are increasingly dependent on Freudian themes. Also, he evolved over the years a style of the utmost simplicity that was particularly suitable for delineating the turgid emotions of his outwardly naïve characters.

Ultimately, it can be seen that the range of Anderson's work is a very narrow one; perversion and desire are themes that he uses again and again, and frustration is another. But this last is important; for the frustration that Anderson dealt with was the frustration of the character who felt choked by the routine of the industrialized life he was leading. Like Anderson himself, many of these characters walked out and found all the happiness they were ever likely to find in an itinerant poverty rather than a static security. It was another example of the writer's apprehension of unease—the moral unease that underlay the insistent dinning of the age of materialism. However narrow his range he does at least reveal a bit of America's psychological illness; and through his personal association with William Faulkner and Scott Fitzgerald he ensured that his apprehension should be perpetuated.

IV

The Negro literature which may be said to have tentatively established itself in the late eighteenth century with the verses of Jupiter Hammon and Phillis Wheatley may seem to have been an unconscionable time arising if one forgets that in the interim of rather more than a century before its development there had been a Civil War of which the moral issue of the Negro's status had been the main cause. There had been other factors, too, that had stimulated its growth: illiteracy and the journalistic dissemination of the Uncle Remus attitude of writers like Joel Chandler Harris and Thomas Nelson Page being the obvious ones. So that for a hundred years there had been nothing but the physical presence of the race, plus a few verses and spirituals and the memory of some oratory of abolition times, to remind white people that a colour problem existed, one that theoretically had been solved by the war but in practice existed still. And the absence of a Negro literature had inevitably meant a naturally biased interpretation of the issues involved, since it was always in the literature of white men that the problem was aired.

This condition was to obtain effectively until after the 1914–18 war, when Negro literature came into its own to the extent of having half a dozen native exponents. The only important Negro writer before the war, if one can in this case consider importance as implying celebrity, was the educationist Booker T. Washington, whose autobiography, *Up From Slavery*, did in fact become world famous. Other than Washington only a few regional writers attained a small local notoriety, e.g. William Dubois with his cultural works and Charles Chesnutt with his novels and short stories, both of whom dealt with racial prejudice soberly and without irony and bitterness.

But the Negro race had not been neglected by white writers of a calibre rather greater than the J. Harris school. Gertrude Stein's story, *Melanctha Herbert*, has already been mentioned; Eugene O'Neill, the playwright, examined the race problem in several of his plays (to be dealt with in the next chapter); Mrs Beecher Stowe is popularly supposed to have precipitated the Civil War with *Uncle Tom's Cabin*; and Sherwood Anderson worked at the problem at the primitivistic level. All these writers were radicals and reformers—as was Dreiser—in a general sense. They were sincere enough to wish to do something about racial prejudice, if only to make it explicit, but that did not prove them to understand the problem deeply enough to pontificate on it. And to aid that understanding a genuine Negro literature was essential.

The eloquence of Booker T. Washington was a splendid beginning, for it was the practical eloquence of the educationist who sees that nothing can be achieved without literacy and work and who himself established the settlement in Alabama where his people made and erected their own buildings and farmed their own land. But Washington's was by no means a radical policy: he disapproved of both college education and government representation for Negroes, and he was very much a Southern traditionalist in the sense that he constantly reminded his people that they had obligations as well as rights. But the slave mentality was rapidly becoming anathema to the twentieth-century generations of Negroes. The folklore symbol of John Henry, the personification of Negro fortitude and physical strength was too deep-rooted ever to be forgotten; but now the time was coming when it must be superseded. The humility of servitude had for too long been confused with the dignity of service; and William Dubois was strongly opposed to the policy of racial submission.

Dubois, like Gertrude Stein, had been a pupil of William James at Harvard. He was himself a New Englander who visited the South for the first time while a student and had his first taste of racial prejudice in active form on seeing the 'jim-crow' rules in operation and the sadistic bewitchery of the Klu-Klux-Klan ill suppressed by the Act of 1871. He realized that education must go much further than Booker Washington thought, and began forthwith to fight for the intensive education of those Negroes who showed the potentialities of leaders, at the same time seeking to establish Negro art and literature on a firm footing. His magazine, *The Crisis*, ran from 1910 to 1934 and was devoted to Negro art on a critical level.

It was Dubois who influenced the expansion of the Harlem district of New York when the Southern Negroes migrated there in thousands during the 1914–18 war, Dubois who through his critical support ensured that the Negro arts of painting, music and sculpture were adequately established for the benefit of the incoming surge of Negroes whose story he had told in *The Souls of Black Folk*, Dubois who was the idol of the younger Negro generation.

Even Dubois, however, could not bring to flowering a complex art like literature until the young men he consistently encouraged in *The Crisis* had become articulate; and this did not begin to happen to any extent until the nineteen-twenties. But by that time Harlem had its own newspapers and magazines and an esoteric racial glory in which top-line vaudeville star and street-corner tout alike could share. It had become the centre of the Negro culture of the world and was rapidly becoming a place of interest to New York residents and visitors—though not, apparently, arousing the kind of interest that would have inspired action to bring rent and wage levels to those obtaining for whites who worked and lived in the same district. But there was no doubt that the post-war intelligentsia found Harlem exciting; and the Negro, inspired by racial glory, lost no time in proving his ability to excite. There is a good dispassionate study of the Negro in Harlem in *Nigger Heaven*, a novel by the essayist and sometime music critic of the *New York Times*, Carl Van Vechten. *Nigger Heaven* is a story of injustice; but Van Vechten rightly shows in his story of an intelligent Negro who suffers for the crimes of an animalistic Negro murderer that injustice is not the prerogative of the white race. Van Vechten's sympathetic but unsentimental treatment of the Negro in *Nigger Heaven* proves him to be one of the sincerest white writers on the subject prior to the arrival of the Faulknerian epics of the 'thirties.

The school of Negro writing that began to come into its own in the post-war period was still a very small one; there was still no Negro writer of stature; but at least the Negro voice was to be heard.

Langston Hughes' words could be heard literally, for

he wrote many verses which were set by the famous jazz musicians of Harlem and Chicago to 'Blues' tunes, as well as two novels of some power, *Not Without Laughter* and *The Ways of White Folks*. His poems are characterized by vivid imagery and primitive rhythms.

Claude McKay, a West Indian, was a little earlier in period, having published his poems, *Songs of Jamaica*, in 1912; but it was Frank Harris the English friend (and sometime enemy) of Shaw and Wilde and discoverer of more talent than he could cope with who elevated McKay to literary importance and saw him established as literary editor of *The Liberator*. McKay was active in all stages of the post-war development of Negro literature. He saw it as his duty not only to write but to get others of his race to write for him and he became one of the most dynamic figures in Harlem. His own novel, *Home To Harlem*, is founded on his experiences as a Pullman porter, and his sonnets express the hopes and fears of his race with some beauty; but it was as an editor that he was most successful.

James Weldon Johnson, who was killed in a New England motor accident in 1938, is remembered chiefly for his Negro anthem *Lift Every Voice and Sing* and Jean Toomer for his miscellany of stories and verse, *Cane*.

The best—and most prolific—of the Negro poets was Countee Cullen who died, too young, in 1946. Cullen was of a generation that voiced its protest against racial discrimination by daring to be cynical about God as well as man:

> I doubt not God is good, well-meaning, kind,
> And did he stoop to quibble could tell why
> The little buried mole continues blind,
> Why flesh that mirrors Him must some day die,
> Make plain the reason tortured Tantalus
> Is baited by the fickle fruit, declare
> If merely brute caprice dooms Sisyphus
> To struggle up a never-ending stair.

Inscrutable his ways are, and immune
To catechism by a mind too strewn
With petty cares to slightly understand
What awful brain compels His awful hand
Yet do I marvel at this curious thing:
To make a poet black, and bid him sing!

A lot of his verse protests with a too-obvious bitterness that weakens its purpose, and self-pity is sometimes too marked to be overlooked; but in lyrics such as *The Love Tree*

Come, let us plant our love as farmers plant
A seed, and you shall water it with tears,
And I shall weed it with my hands until
They bleed. Perchance this buried love of ours
Will fall on goodly ground and bear a tree
With fruit and flowers; pale lovers chancing here
May pluck and eat, and through their veins a sweet
And languid ardour play, their pulses beat
An unimagined tune, their shy lips meet
And part, and bliss repeat again. And men
Will pilgrimage from far and wide to see
This tree for which we two were crucified,
And, happy in themselves, will never know
'Twas break of heart that made the Love Tree grow

he shows a good rhythmic sense and a pleasant *naïveté* that just—perhaps only just—avoids being dewy-eyed. Cullen almost certainly wrote too much and repeated himself too many times, but in isolated lines and stanzas he attains considerable poetic stature.

These Negro writers were all dwarfed in stature technically (though by no means belittled aesthetically) by Richard Wright, who was born in Natchez, Mississippi, in 1908. Wright is generally recognized as the greatest Negro writer today and can justly be compared with Dreiser, from whom he learnt the technique of Naturalism. He has told of his own terrified youth in *Black Boy*, published in 1945, and extended that atmosphere of oppression into a history of Negro persecution in *Twelve Million Black Voices*; but his greatest work to date is the novel *Native Son* (1940).

This is a long and tragic tale of a Negro murderer whose environmental confusion breeds ruthlessness within him. Because it is sanely and powerfully told and uses all the naturalistic skill Wright had absorbed from Dreiser it has the cathartic effect that is the test of true tragedy. And once again something is added to the uniqueness of American literature: the voice of the Negro burdened with the symptoms of racial distress.

V

The enveloping materialism of the twentieth century, interpreted by the realists of literature who contrived in the prophetic manner of the artist always to keep a little ahead of the envelopment, naturally did not go unchallenged. In the main, reaction took two forms: a reversion to classicism and a purely escapist romanticism. The classicism was by no means well founded, for America knew nothing of classic traditions; and the romanticism was by no means the heightening of imaginative powers to be associated with Melville. Both were, rather, straws to be clutched by those who saw the danger of drift but could only dig their toes in and point out that in a world gone mad anyone going in the opposite direction from the masses was bound to appear wrong.

T. S. Eliot, escaping into classicism, found it necessary to forsake America and seek a more sophisticated world in Europe. From Oxford, the Sorbonne, the city banking house and the Bloomsbury publisher's office he was able to view with proper objectivity the melée in the country of his birth. By 1915, when he settled in England, the World War was in progress and decadence was clearly beyond arrest; but at least he could show the perceptive few who understood his allusions that here was no hope, that

> Death and the Raven drift above
> And Sweeney guards the hornèd gate.

Eliot's poems have had a profound influence on almost the entire range of literature in English. Technically, in verse and verse drama, he has overcome what might have been a purely esoteric appeal by adapting the rhythms of ordinary speech and by disguising his genuine profundity behind a façade that is immediately attractive to the snob element of the middle classes. But he has never been, in the unique sense, an American. His voice is lofty and remote in spite of the enormous audience he has gathered to himself and he has firmly stated that

> What is to be insisted upon is that the poet must develop or procure the consciousness of the past and that he should continue to develop this consciousness throughout his career.

And so with his roots in the classic past he stands, offering a refuge from the onward-ever-onward snowball of materialism—a refuge from which the bystander can view the waste land and spit, safe in the knowledge that he at least hasn't joined in the mad rush to doom.

But if Eliot offers no unique American qualities, James Branch Cabell, firmly establishing his reactionary tent in the Romantic camp, certainly does. For his work, with its recurring phallic symbolism is now seen to be symptomatic of the intense preoccupation with sensuality that has characterized the average American male's professed horror of homosexuality. 'Virility, virility—all is virility; and let no one mention the pansy at my feet'—this seems to be the firebreath warning emitted by Young Male America today; but indeed no one would have questioned his virility if he hadn't drawn attention to it himself by falling over backwards in his effort to dodge the blow that was never aimed. But now that one's attention has been drawn one begins to raise a questioning eyebrow with regard to his girlishly influenced clothes and his delight in vulgar jewelry. However, one can accept the aggressive masculinity as a national characteristic even if the school that interprets it often has small literary value.

Cabell has had much to do—though possibly unintentionally—with the establishment of that school.

Born in Virginia in 1879, he has ostensibly led the life of a patrician Southern gentleman and scholar, frequently pontificating on what should be America's attitude to art with a very big A:

> . . . you perceive, I trust, that your personal indifference, and the lazy contempt of America as a whole, toward art matters no more effects the eternal verity and the eternal importance of art than do the religious practices of Abyssinia, say, effect the verity and importance of the New Testament. You perceive, I trust, that you ought to be interested in art matters, whatever is your actual emotion.

But he himself had done little more toward the widening of art's horizon than inspire a number of unimportant entertainers to take up the cudgels on behalf of a Romanticism they little understand and less appreciate, in the pages of countless glossy magazines. Those pages have for so long now remained the hideout of a spurious Romanticism and a coy sentimentalism that one is apt to forget that it is in them as much as anywhere that the qualities of spuriousness and sentimentality have been perpetuated and now emerge as facets of the American character.

Cabell first won recognition as a stylist, but his style is in fact often open to reproach and the critics who hailed him were almost certainly taken in by his penchant for Wildean epigrams, e.g. 'The Religion of Hell is patriotism, and the government is an enlightened democracy.' Cabell may have a natural wit, but his style derives in the main from a curious assembly of mentors—Shaw, Stevenson, J. M. Synge, George Moore and Wilde being easily detectable. He sets most of his romantic fantasies in the imaginary territory of Poictesme and peoples them with lovers, chevaliers, figures half stolen from classical mythology and half imagined, queens, knights and ladies-of-the-grail. But always there is the attempt to prove that by acts of valour and loyalty man is *ipso facto* a courageous and loyal creature and that, as Cabell himself says,

> . . . romance has invariably been the demiurgic and beneficent force, not merely in letters, but in every matter which concerns mankind; and . . . realism with its teaching that the mile-posts along the road are as worthy of consideration as the goal, has always figured as man's chief enemy.

In *Jurgen*, his best-known work, Cabell pretends to attack middle-class materialism with satirical arrows shot from the ivory tower of classicism; but his self-conscious naughtiness and phoney intellectualism make a poor showing beside T. S. Eliot's profound observations. However, it is the Cabell brand of Romanticism that has influenced those writers who have wanted to cash in on the people's desire to escape from the everyday cares of materialism by offering them romantic dreams of hair-on-the-chest masculinity refined by rogueish chivalry. Those dreams will stand little inspection in a strong literary light; but there is not much doubt of their importance as a symptom of the American's capacity for delusion.

CHAPTER SEVEN

The Pace of Living and the Growth of Literature

I

JUST as in medicine there is a continual search for the antidote to every infection, so in literature it is part of the business of the critic to draw attention to tendencies he views as weakening to literature as a whole. It is the creative writer who has to find and administer the corrective. But the writer who has been guilty of weakening the structure may in fact have been reflecting a moral weakness he has perceived in humanity. It is another part of the business of the critic to evaluate and decide.

From Poe onwards the American critics have shown the proper lively and intelligent interest in their national literature; but they have proved themselves more than simply competent. Perhaps because theirs is a young literature they have been less influenced by the dead wood of criticism—the fashionable phrases, the cant that pleads the virtue of the past, the stupidities pretending to be ideas that are too often perpetuated by critics who have no ideas of their own, and all the jargon that has accumulated round English literary criticism since medieval times.

Unfortunately the many excellent American critics cannot usefully be enumerated and discussed in a survey as concise as this one. The general reader may be familiar with a few names—H. L. Mencken, George Jean Nathan, Van Wyck Brooks, Maxwell Geismar, Edmund Wilson, Lionel Trilling, Joseph Warren Beach, Cleanth Brooks and Malcom Cowley will probably have crossed his horizon from time to time; but he is unlikely to be enlightened further by the few words that could here be given to individual studies of these critics. Although criticism is a creative activity it hasn't the immediate value of the literature it is criticizing, which is in its turn offering a criticism of life, because clearly it can concern itself only with what has been written; and it therefore seems best when space is limited to concentrate on the tendencies themselves rather than the critics' evaluation of them. But it must be pointed out that, in the twentieth century particularly, the critics have often created the atmosphere in which experimental or adventurous writing could flourish. Often they have done more than merely exert their critical force; many of them have been instrumental in persuading publishers to accept books by unknown authors. And many of them achieved a personal fame—as Arnold Bennett did in England—that made their pronouncements awe inspiring if not actually inviolable.

II

It is easy to forget that not all literature achieves the permanency of books. The ephemeral nature of periodicals detracts from their indicative qualities when one is considering literary trends. But it is worth noting that, even if newspapers are excluded, the audience for periodic literature is still a vast one. And in a country the size of America it is also worth noting that the periodical is still the most effective—and most expensive—form of advertising.

A few of the journals adopting critical standards were mentioned at the end of Chapter Three. That short list could be lengthened considerably to include the titles of journals that have introduced the work of every major English-language writer to American audiences. But the importance of another kind of periodical must be touched on.

This is the much-denigrated magazine, in all its infinite glossy variety, that was originally a journal of instruction and genteel entertainment. The literary journal had also been genteel and instructive originally, and certainly remained instructive; but in accordance with the increasing pace of living resulting from industrialization the magazine broke away from critical standards and became informative and entertaining on another, slicker, level.

The slickness was of course in itself an indication of the increasing pace of living. There was little leisure now to indulge one's fancy as a literary gent, even though the new pace of life was paradoxically intended to secure increased leisure, for all one's time was spent in commuting and in trying to keep in step with a generation of people who had never known leisure and were interested in it only to the extent of filling it with pursuits more active than literature. In theory, of course, 'all that sort of thing' was taken care of in the new education, but in practice it was quickly abandoned on leaving college.

It is in the period 1900–30 that the influence of such writers as James Branch Cabell, O. Henry, Booth Tarkington and Peter B. Kyne can be seen to be having its effect. Although the most go-getting individual in the world, the American of the first thirty years of the twentieth century wanted to be reminded of his direction as little as possible. Any kind of literature that pulled him up with a jolt and set him in front of a looking-glass was at least unbelievable. He was perfectly willing to call himself 'radical' and 'reforming,' but at least one foot must be cemented to the playground of romantic escapism. And if that romantic escapism had a touch of the scholarly about it he could enjoy the upstage world of the literary gent too.

Cabell's work has been discussed. It didn't actually get

into the glossy magazines because of its eroticism and because it fooled even critics of the stature of Mencken (*Harper's Magazine* and the *American Mercury* were fooled too). But it struck a note that others were striking for oncoming writers to pipe their tunes to.

Of those who struck stridently while Cabell was still tentatively testing the gong, William Sidney Porter, pseudonymously known as O. Henry, must receive a mention if only for the reason that he is still the only American writer known to a good many English readers today and because his technical methods are enthroned in perpetuity for the benefit of students of correspondence schools.

Porter is famous for his ah!-that's-life philosophy and for the trick endings to his stories. His attitude to life is that of the gentle observer with the smile that always just escapes being cynical—the observer who realizes full well that life offers more kicks than ha'pence but would like you to know that the ha'pence are well worth the kicks; his trick endings are skilful in the extreme but, as with Maupassant's *The Necklace*, one too often feels that the tales have gone through procrustean handling for the sake of giving the reader a surprise.

The argument in favour of Porter's retention as an important literary figure is that where his surprise endings offer no repeatable pleasure his philosophy does. But his philosophy is too dependent on half-truths to be useful. For example, his most famous story, *The Gifts of the Magi*, tells of a husband and wife in poor circumstances each of whom sacrifices a cherished possession to buy the other a heart's-desire Christmas gift—only to find that by one of life's little ironies each is worse off than before. For the wife sells her hair to enable her to buy a chain for her husband's watch, while he meanwhile sells the watch to buy his wife a comb for her hair. If the point Porter intended to make is that fate is ironical, then he has forced his irony into such a shapely shape that it lacks verisimilitude, and once again the reader is left with the surprise of the ending as his sole reward.

There is of course a highly commendable skill involved in such technical tricks—an inimitable skill that requires a certain kind of mind for its performance—in short, a knack that is most entertaining. The trouble begins when the knack is confused with a deep perception of life.

Porter has had many imitators and equals in the sphere of his spurious philosophy; and although spurious philosophies are not by any means restricted to the twentieth century—one has only to recall the maidenly twitterings of James Gates Percival in the previous one—it certainly happened that Porter and his imitators had everything in common with the age. Soon so many authors were imitating him in the pages of the 'glossies' (not only in America but in England too), and with such success, that the quality of their spuriousness, never exaggerated to the stage where it becomes easy to parody like Victorian melodrama, began to convince by repetition, like propaganda. And in a way it was propaganda—propaganda for the way of life that is moving too fast to know its own direction.

Behind the acceptance of this kind of escapism, which has continued to the present day, there seems to lie a fear of life itself. That would have to be discussed at a philosophical level outside the scope of this book. At a purely literary level it reflects the reactionary view of Cabell quoted in the previous chapter. But although such writing is sometimes said to be responsible for the continuation of a *milieu* in which realistic writers have no chance, it is in fact often the *raison d'être* of the anguish in which realists and genuine romanticists find their motivation. And although such spurious literature proves that even if literature is always getting bigger it isn't necessarily getting better, it is at least a very definite reflexion of the temper of the times, and as such has its value.

III

The commercialization and deliberate superficiality of the basically reactionary force that controlled the glossy magazine world of the twentieth century had been at work in the American theatre long before 1900. Actually the drama as such can hardly be said to have had any existence in America prior to 1900. The nineteenth century had its eclectic productions derived from the English theatre (itself in a state of doldrums creatively); but before that the Puritan influence had been too strong for drama to penetrate the public conscience. So although many theatres were built in all the new cities that sprang up as railways and big business opened up the continent, there was nothing of any merit to be seen in them. Writers who turned to the theatre usually did so with get-rich-quick motives and catchpenny ideas aimed at equally catchpenny audiences. The theatre was a complete success as a commercial proposition (with millions of money invested in it) and an utter failure as a medium for art.

In Europe as the nineteenth century closed the dramatic renascence begun by Ibsen was gathering impetus. Helped by playwrights like Shaw and Hauptmann and Synge public interest in the revival had become intense. It was an interest elaborated by conflict and public outcries and it was all the theatre needed to become a creative force again. The problem play, the expressionist play, the folklore play, the impressionist play, the naturalistic play, the symbollic play: *in toto*, these offered the complete incentive. Playwrights reintroduced elements that had not been used for centuries; structure was torn to pieces and rebuilt, formal dialogue was abandoned, scenery was elaborated, music brought in, lighting used with new effect. It might be said that a new beginning was made in which only the basic assumptions of an audience and some actors were considered.

This excitement was not long crossing the Atlantic. In 1906 William Vaughan Moody, a poet from Indiana who was far from parochial in his outlook and who had crossed the Atlantic many times in the course of his acquisition of a cosmopolitan culture, turned his attention to the commercial theatre. Moody had already written a trilogy of poetic dramas, but these were of the kind not intended for acting, though they were none the less something of an achievement; but in *The Great Divide* there was ample evidence that his residence in Europe had not been without result and that he had learnt all he needed to know about the technique of drama. This, plus Moody's natural interest in psychological problems, made *The Great Divide* an extraordinarily powerful play. The theme is that of the girl with the Puritan upbringing who has to face attempted seduction and agrees to marrying one of her would-be seducers as an alternative to the violation her conscience rejects. Her subsequent shame comes between her and her husband (whom she has come genuinely to love) and its expiation forms the main conflict of the play.

Although the realism of Ibsen had its little day in the work of American playwrights such as James Herne, whose gloomy domestic tragedies were at least inspiriting so far as newness of outlook was concerned, drama turned down the psychological path, whither it was led by Moody, and opened out into the vast dark vistas of Eugene O'Neill's complete works.

O'Neill was born in New York in 1888, was educated unpretentiously at various schools while his parents, both actors, were on road tours, and ended that period of formal education at Princeton, from which he graduated in 1906. He knocked about the world for the next ten years, got himself married and divorced and contracted tuberculosis. After being discharged from the Connecticut sanitorium to which he had been sent for rest and treatment, O'Neill experimented with the writing of a number of one-act plays, subsequently published privately (which publication was paid for by O'Neill senior) and produced by a New York repertory group, The Princeton Players. None of these plays is important except as an indication of the direction in which O'Neill was moving, and indeed they have been excluded by the author from his collected works. But in 1919 another collection of one-act plays was published, and this included *The Moon of the Caribees*, an elemental piece on an extremely animalistic level, in which O'Neill introduces Negro characters—though not to investigate their psychology as he did in 1920 in *The Emperor Jones*.

Admittedly *The Emperor Jones* is nothing like so profoundly Freudian as O'Neill's later plays were to become, because in it O'Neill was experimenting with dramatic methods of communicating the emotion of fear that forms the heart of the play; but it does attempt to show the sophisticated Negro emperor's reversion to inherent savagery when pursued by his rebellious people.

It was actually to be some years before O'Neill was completely successful in the psychological drama. In the meantime he experimented in every possible direction; indeed the whole corpus of his work is concerned with experimentation.

Anna Christie was awarded the Pulitzer Prize for 1922—an award of dubious merit, but in this case fairly bestowed for O'Neill's determination to instil some resemblance of reality into the commercial theatre. It is a play in which a proper balance between squalor and sentimentality has not been arrived at—or perhaps even visualized; but it has a curious rhythmic power, and in its attempt to portray the regenerate harlot daughter of a bargemaster in all the blowsiness of her character it has many moments that are genuinely moving.

O'Neill always showed a deep concern for the racial problem of the Negro and in *All God's Chillun Got Wings* he dealt subtly and realistically with the situation of inter-racial marriage. But almost immediately he left this problem for another—a study of the incestuous lust resulting from the inbreeding of a New England poor-white family. *Desire Under the Elms* was an immense success on Broadway, but in the main this success must be attributed to its sensational indecency rather than to its value as drama. The play shows O'Neill's clear understanding of the motivations of lustful violence, but makes almost impossible demands on traditional acting technique and is certainly better to read than to watch, for in a leisured reading one is not constantly whipped into a state of spurious emotion by the characters' crude and painful antics and there is time to observe how very deep is O'Neill's perception. It is perhaps his greatest fault as a dramatist that he is continually making demands that the conventions of the proscenium stage are not fitted to satisfy. So many of his plays failed because he was apparently unsure of his direction. In fact O'Neill was always quite sure which way he wanted to go: his failure lay in not understanding that the dramatist must work within the limits of his medium. But that failing was magnificent in its imaginative scope, and when O'Neill's experiments came off they added something to the literature of the theatre.

The most successful of these experiments was in *Strange Interlude*, in which the audience is concerned not only with the characters' overt intentions but with their thoughts and their inner lives too. Here is a brilliant—though overlong—exposition of the Freudian theory of frustration.

Strange Interlude deals with the repressed sexual desires of Nina Leeds, whose marriage to a soldier was not consummated before he was killed in action. Nina feels that she has failed him because she allowed her father to deter her from consummation, and in expiation of her sin she offers her body lavishly to the inmates of a home for wounded soldiers. But there is no satisfaction for her in this brutal promiscuity and she must needs get married again, to a very young man who arouses the maternal instinct in her and forms a link with her dead husband, whose idolator he was. This situation is only the beginning of a play in which hereditary insanity, abortion, nymphomania and divorce form the developing elements. It is a play that runs for nine acts and takes at least two evenings to perform. It is a play in which seemingly every kind of neurosis is exposed and investigated; it is certainly much more a psychiatric case history than a drama in accepted terms; but in spite of what must seem in précis to be unutterably dreary and boring the play holds the interest in performance because of its quite comprehensible analysis of mental subtleties.

In *Mourning Becomes Electra* O'Neill retells the Æschylean story of Agamemnon and Electra, choosing the Civil War as his setting. This tortuous investigation of the morbid owes something in atmosphere to Poe, and in dramatic construction to the Elizabethan dramatists Webster and Marlowe rather than to Æschylus; but it has also something of the inevitability of Shakespearean tragedy in its conflict of tremendous forces. *Mourning Becomes Electra* is a triology of plays requiring extended performance, and for that reason is seldom given today; but it is certainly the highest point of O'Neill's achievement in the sphere of emotional drama.

In philosophical exploration O'Neill has made one or two noteworthy achievements, though they have not been attended by conspicuous success commercially. *The Great God Brown* and *Lazarus Laughed* puzzled audiences mainly, perhaps, because of the symbolic use of masks. Once again O'Neill had unwarrantably presumed a perception his audiences did not possess. But there is no doubt of the value of these two plays. *Lazarus* is a beautifully wrought fantasy based on the idea that only in death can the fullness of life be appreciated. Lazarus, resurrected by Christ from his glimpse beyond the grave, is placed in opposition to the cruelty of Caligula's court and to the inherent rottenness of the Roman civilization, and the laughter that symbolizes the faith he has been able to prove justified is shown as capable of raising to a state of ecstasy the squalor of the court. The use of masks, music, mime, ballet and static grouping seems to indicate that O'Neill here wanted to combine all the arts in a single entertainment.

If one considers the whole of O'Neill's work for the stage in an effort to make some kind of assessment of its total value, one is faced with a very difficult task; for there is no static viewpoint adopted by the playwright in any big proportion of his work. The Nietschean doctrine of *Lazarus Laughed* is balanced by the geniality of his most popular play *Ah! Wilderness*; the animal lusts of *Desire Under the Elms* makes nonsense of the outpouring of love and forgiveness in *Days Without End*. There is of course no reason why an author should not progress from one point of view to another as the result of his experience of life; and this is in fact what very often happens. But in the case of Eugene O'Neill there seems very little possibility of deciding which was in fact the line of his achievement. The chronological order of the plays is less indicative with O'Neill than with any other dramatist of note. Almost every play he wrote is an achievement in its own sphere;

and perhaps the only assessment that can sensibly be made is that his technical curiosity was always a little out of step with his reasoning. Like Theodore Dreiser, he was a man who could not make up his mind; but, unlike the novelist, his confusion did not make him take refuge in an inflated nihilism. He believed, ultimately, in too many things, and the inevitable tendency, when seen in perspective, was for each to cancel out the other. But there can be no doubt at all that his mind was the most alert in the theatre of the twentieth century and his creative power undiminished when he died in 1954.

Of the American playwrights whose stature is in various ways comparable with O'Neill's, Sidney Howard, Philip Barry, Paul Green and Marc Connelly matured creatively rather later. Howard's *The Silver Cord* was produced in 1926, Connelly's beautiful fantasy of the Negro's conception of heaven *Green Pastures* in 1930, Green's tragic folk tale *In Abraham's Bosom* in 1926, and Barry's *Paris Bound* in 1927. All these playwrights have been careful to preserve some semblance of popular appeal in their work. This quality—which O'Neill so studiously ignored except in *Ah! Wilderness* and *Strange Interlude*—naturally helped to ensure their commercial success; but this must naturally not be taken as in any way denigrating work of inestimable value in the brief history of the drama in America. In every Western country that produces art there is always a body of opinion that tips its nose at popular success and is precious enough to believe that nothing worth while ever drew a big audience. Such cliques take a delight in an O'Neill for quite the wrong reasons and profess to scorn the Barrys and Howards and Connellys from equally faulty reasoning. O'Neill's immense scope deployed his interest over qualities that were of greater concern to him than commercial success; other dramatists, aiming from shorter range, were able to hit the target more frequently.

But it is quite wrong to play them off against each other for this reason alone.

In later years the work of Clifford Odets, Tennessee Williams and Maxwell Anderson on the naturalistic level, of Thornton Wilder in the purlieus of metaphysics, and William Saroyan in the realm of the most naïve romanticism has achieved considerable popularity.

Odets' plays *Waiting for Lefty* and *Awake and Sing* were both products of the years of depression prior to the Second World War. *Awake and Sing* is unquestionably the finer of the two; but both attempt an awakening of a sense of social justice by methods that seemed revolutionary then and are indubitably dated now. As with the 'leftist' presentations by the Unity Theatre group in the London of the same period, they served their purpose and went their way, proving by their passing that their themes were not durable. In his post-war plays *Winter Journey* and *The Big Knife* Odets has proved himself to be still too dependent on mechanical situations that are capable of inflation to convincing proportions—when acted and produced as finely as Sam Wanamaker can act and produce them. So long as one is in the theatre watching them one suspends disbelief with ease; but in recollection there appears a curious hollow where a heart should lie, and one can think of these melodramas of fallen actors and blackmailed film stars only as glossy inflations of very ordinary magazine stories; and the gloss seems curiously susceptible to mildew.

Maxwell Anderson was born in the same year as Eugene O'Neill (1888) and, like him, has experimented enthusiastically with old and new devices of stagecraft to achieve his ends. *Winterset*, his most famous play, is based on the Sacco-Vanzetti case and sets out to prove that only at the cost of human lives can some value be extracted from a situation in which misplaced justice is the key. *High Tor*, like a later play, *Thunder Rock* by Robert Ardrey, is based on a visionary experience which changes the life and moral outlook of the protagonist. In *High Tor* there is as strong a sense of optimism as there is of pessimism in the earlier play; and in *Star Wagon* the visionary future is projected into the lives of a group instead of an individual. There can be no doubt about Maxwell Anderson's ability to hold the interest of his audience, but in retrospect it is seen to be an ability that perhaps depends a little too much on novelty and stagecraft for their own sakes.

Tennessee Williams's best-known plays, *The Glass Menagerie* and *A Streetcar Named Desire*, are both very definitely poetic works based on the idea of the eternal conflict between the mind and the spirit. Various characters are shown in a juxtaposition that arises from their individual concern with reality and illusion. It is the inability of the characters whose lives are spun out in a world of the imagination to adjust themselves to the demands of reality that forms the conflict of Williams's plays. They are plays in which every character is marvellously realized; but as in the plays of Clifford Odets there is a tendency to assume that only in terms of the most obvious melodrama can audiences be expected to cope with such subtle themes. There is justice in the assumption, but it does not make for the quality of durability in any play. Although it may be heretical to say so, there are strong grounds for believing that Williams's most enduring work is his delicately perceptive novel *The Roman Spring of Mrs Stone*. Once again, here are the worlds of reality and imagination in conflict, but there is no attempt to bestow on the story a corny symbolism that can be understood by millions, and for that reason it lacks the vulgarity that makes the intention of *A Streetcar Named Desire* so obvious. But Tennessee Williams is still a young man and, having cornered his audience, he may yet offer them a play of greater value.

Thornton Wilder was famous for his short novel *The*

Bridge of San Luis Rey a whole decade before he put *Our Town* on the stage and showed that the abolition of scenery and properties tended to heighten the effect of mystery that surrounds the destiny of man. In *The Skin of Our Teeth* he reverted to the stage conventions of realism only to show how irrelevant such conventions are. As the play proceeds the audience have the conventions denounced before their very eyes as actors are replaced by theatre staff, scenery is moved about in accordance with the would-be actors' whims, and all kinds of stage illusions are done away with. The morality play that forms the backbone of this strange to-do is concerned with no one time or place: the age of the dinosaur, the age of Napoleon, the present day and the future are all telescoped into one, and the Antrobus family are seen to be symbolic of the family of mankind.

The advantage of allegory is of course that it has a universal appeal—at any rate among people who are willing to go rather more than a few steps away from the doorstep of theatrical conventions. This was proved when *The Skin of Our Teeth* was presented in many of the cities of Europe in transliterated versions and invariably became a great success.

Thornton Wilder is a Christian Humanist whose most intense preoccupation is with ethical problems. The destiny of mankind, as distinct from his own personal destiny, is for him the all-absorbing question. In this he may be compared with Melville; but, as has been seen, Melville was an unself-conscious artist who was not even aware that he was writing tales of allegorical significance. Wilder is the metaphysician who knowingly brings his carefully wrought literary technique to bear on his ethical ideas. He is a dispassionate artist and for that reason may appear a little bloodless; but there can be no doubt of his sincerity.

William Saroyan, on the other hand, is always so artless that one very soon begins to have grave doubts not only of his sincerity but his intelligence too. His pipe dreams of human benevolence are clearly based on the most romantic kind of wishful thinking rather than on actual observation, and all his people are so good that they very soon appear to be thoroughly dislikable. For example, in his play *The Time of Your Life* the stage is peopled the whole time with curious eccentrics who appear to have nothing to do but delight in their own absurdities; and evil, when it appears in the shape of a corrupt policeman, is vanquished by the incorruptible light of good that radiates from the water-front saloon's inhabitants. In the collections of plays generically entitled *The Beautiful People* the same kind of maudlin benevolence motivates all the plots; and surrounding the benevolence is an aura of what is apparently intended to be poetic fantasy but which seems to have no special relevance.

All this faith in the essential goodness of humanity is no doubt laudable in theory, but when tricked out with so much god-wottery it tends to become nauseating. Saroyan began his literary career as a short-story writer, and in that category of literature he achieves a greater success, for the burden of so much goodness is more easily borne in the few pages of a short story than in the three-hours' traffic of the stage. Saroyan is the typical market-place spieler, raconteur, who holds and interests with his somewhat pointless anecdotes for a moment or two and then is gone, leaving the pinchbeck watch or the cure-all draught of human kindness dangling in the customer's hand and with exhortations to belief still ringing in his ears. It is only when the customer moves away out of the market-place and looks at the tarnishing metal that he realizes that once more he has been caught by a phoney tale and that anyway he isn't after all so very interested in so Utopian a tale of human nature. It seems too from his later work that Saroyan's small skill, inflated beyond its capacity by a curiously Victorian morality is languishing into mere repetition and that in fact all he had to say was contained within the covers of his first book of short stories *The Daring Young Man on the Flying Trapeze*.

In summary, it will be clear that in the category of drama there has so far been no emergence of any essentially American quality comparable to that of the novel and the poem. Eugene O'Neill towers above all other dramatists who happen to be American by birth, but, although his work undoubtedly has the quality of universality in its themes, it has failed, on the whole, in extracting any specific significance from the American way of life and projecting it on to the stage. That task is still to be attempted. It appears, in 1954, that the essentially American contribution to the stage may be sidetracked into the field of the spectacular 'musical,' and one is happy for this to be so, for it is a field that has been ill explored by other nations since the passing of Gilbert and Sullivan. But in 1954 American drama of any quality at all is still only fifty years old. It is a very short time in which to expect the emergence of uniqueness.

IV

It might be thought that the pace of living in the twentieth century would stultify the natural growth of poetry, which is sometimes believed to demand a more epicurean atmosphere to flourish in. But this has not proved to be the case, for the simple reason that poetry *per se* demands nothing at all except a subject. Certain kinds of poetry may die out because the ways of life they reflect have ceased to exist, but this is merely a matter of fashion or developing thought, not of life-and-death importance.

In America, the influence of scientific thought, of commercialization, of monopolistic enterprise, of the machine age or the age of materialism or whatever one cares to call it, resulted, as has been demonstrated, in the firm establishment in prose and drama of the naturalistic concept of life. After Whitman there was a general tendency to break with the traditions of Romanticism—a break that became more or less complete except for the pockets of resistance formed by the dubious Romanticism cultivated by the magazine writers referred to earlier in this chapter. This break was effective in poetry too, though it naturally took rather longer to become so—poetry being an art that had proved itself peculiarly susceptible to Romanticism in its lyrical aspect.

Perhaps the first poet who needs consideration as an exemplar of the changing mood is one who conveniently published his first verses just four years before the end of the nineteenth century—Edward Arlington Robinson.

Robinson's life was a quiet one and his determination to become a poet was equally unpretentious. He was a civil servant under Theodore Roosevelt's administration, but soon gave up his work to devote his time to poetry. In character he was most admirable—quietly sure of his own merits but genuinely surprised when they were recognized by others. It is true to say that his carefully maintained balance between extremes of thought sometimes results in a lack of passion, but his delineation or character is often touched by irony; and it is as an observer of character that he shares with Browning a special perception.

A melancholy face Charles Carville had,
But not so melancholy as it seemed,
When once you knew him, for his mouth redeemed
His insufficient eyes, forever sad:
In them there was no life-glimpse, good or bad,
No joy, nor passion in them ever gleamed;
His mouth was all of him that ever beamed,
His eyes were sorry, but his mouth was glad.

He never was a fellow that said much,
And half of what he did say was not heard
By many of us: we were out of touch
With all his whims and all his theories
Till he was dead, so those blank eyes of his
Might speak them. Then we heard them every word.

Robinson's portrait gallery of characters is never less than competent, often far more—as, for example, in *Ben Jonson entertains a man from Stratford*, in which he succeeds in something that has seldom been achieved elsewhere—the presentation of Shakespeare as a life-like creature with foibles and vanities that other biographers have often hesitated to add because of misplaced awe.

These portrait poems may be said to indulge Robinson's penchant for realism; but he also wrote a series of Arthurian romances, *Merlin*, *Lancelot* and *Tristram*, and a number of psychological narratives of which *Cavender's House* is perhaps the most successful. In both the legendary stories and the exciting evocations of the grimly haunted house to which the murderer Cavender returns after killing his wife, the poet is successful in establishing the dimensions of genuine tragedy; in both he is concerned with the activities of the mind rather than the body; and all through his work there runs a thread of melancholy that never quite becomes despair. He stands at the beginning of a new century, uncertain as most people of the road he must take, but at least aware that there are several alternatives and that man in his journey can consider all of them:

Where was he going, this man against the sky?
You know not, nor do I.
But this we know, if we know anything:
That we may laugh and fight and sing
And of our transcience here make offering
To an orient Word that will not be erased,
Or, save in incommunicable gleams
Too permanent for dreams,
Be found or known.

He is a little out of fashion now, but there is no American poet who better exemplifies the point of balance between Romance and Naturalism.

Robert Frost, on the other hand, has never become unfashionable, perhaps because his gentle lyricism is concerned more often with nature than with human nature. He too is a New Englander who works in traditional verse forms on themes that are touched by the gentle breath of melancholy:

My sorrow, when she's here with me,
  Thinks these dark days of autumn rain
Are beautiful as days can be;
She loves the bare, the withered tree;
  She walks the sodden pasture lane.

Her pleasure will not let me stay.
  She talks and I am fain to list:
She's glad the birds are gone away,
She's glad her simple worsted grey
  Is silver now with clinging mist.

The desolate, deserted trees,
  The faded earth, the heavy sky,
The beauties she so truly sees,
She thinks I have no eye for these
  And vexes me for reason why.

Not yesterday I learned to know
  The love of bare November days
Before the coming of the snow,
But it were vain to tell her so,
  And they are better for her praise.

But Frost by no means enriches the reader only with his experience as a close observer of man in juxtaposition to nature. That he understands only too well man's superstitious fears will be seen in the poem *The Code*, in which a farm labourer narrates how he tried to murder the employer who had passed an unfavourable remark about his work in the fields. There is no personal rancour in the tale, but one sees immediately that the violation of the local code of honour is more than can be borne by the labourer. For a moment we have been in touch with a pagan fear, and have understood it.

There are lyrical, metaphysical and romantic elements in Frost's poetry, all of them displayed with a technical eloquence that is never less than sure footed. A regionalist by nature, in the tradition of Sarah Orne Jewett, he has become one of the most beloved poets in his own country and surely the best-known American poet in England. Together with Edward Arlington Robinson and Conrad Aiken, Frost helped to steady the ships of radical theme and imagist method that other poets were soon engaged in launching.

The poets who have come to be known by their own wish as the Imagist Group need a brief explanation if one is to understand how they tended to direct the movement of poetry into the narrower and more specialized limits that had constrained it in England during the seventeenth century. They are important not so much for their methods—which were not new—as for their apprehension of the tendency to disintegration of the modern way of life.

This very self-conscious group was led in America by Ezra Pound, who had been influenced by the French symbolists (Verlaine, Rimbaud, Baudelaire, Mallarmé) who in their turn owed much to Poe and his Gothic embroideries. The Imagists were few in number and fortunate in their circumstances, for they had the newly established Chicago magazine *Poetry*, whose guiding star was Harriet Monroe, and the fabulous and fabulously wealthy Amy Lowell to take over the leadership after a quarrel with Ezra Pound, who in any case was far too big a poet to be confined to the narrow limits of a 'movement' for very long. Among them in those early days was Richard Aldington, D. H. Lawrence (in England), Hilda Doolittle (subsequently Mrs Richard Aldington), and John Gould Fletcher; and to these were soon added James Joyce, Ford Madox Ford and William Carlos Williams. The Imagists suffered as well as benefited from the somewhat burdensome organization of Miss Lowell, yet if there was one thing they never lacked it was adequate publicity, and they drew considerable notoriety to themselves with the publication of the Imagist manifesto, which laid down fairly clearly their aims:

1. To employ precisely, and without needless ornament the language of common speech.
2. To create new rhythms, in free verse if necessary, as the expression of new moods.
3. To allow absolute freedom in the choice of subjects.
4. To present an Image.
5. To produce poetry that is hard and clear, never blurred and indefinite.
6. To secure concentration, the very essence of poetry.

If one is to try and typify imagist poetry by a single example from a single poet—as is necessary here—it should be to Hilda Doolittle ('H. D.') that one should turn, for it is she who seems to understand most fully the underlying aims of imagist poetry: not merely that her fellow-Imagists were trying 'to employ precisely . . . the language of common speech,' which could hardly be called a new aim, but that they, and she, were trying to suggest by dilettante methods that there was a destructive force at work in the twentieth-century mind. And the dilettante method was surely right, for it suggests the inward brooding nostalgia that was the secret refuge from the restlessness of the day.

Mid-Day is one of Hilda Doolittle's most perfect short poems; its awareness of defeat is terrifying:

The heat beats upon me
I am startled—
a split leaf crackles on the paved floor.
I am anguished—defeated.
A slight wind shakes the seed-pods—
my thoughts are spent
as the black seeds.
My thoughts tear me,
I dread their fever.
I am scattered in its whirl.
I am scattered like
the hot shrivelled seeds.

The shrivelled seeds
are split in the path—
the grass bends with dust,
the grape slips
under its cracked leaf:
yet far beyond the spent seed-pods,
and the blackened stalks of mint,
the poplar is bright on the hill,
the poplar spreads out,
deep-rooted among trees.

O poplar, you are great
among the hill-stones,
while I perish on the path
among the crevices of the rocks.

Thus mid-day, the burning heat of civilization, the elemental rocks, the world in decline toward the evening.

The Imagists were never uniquely American in their voice: they were simply poets, aware and interpretive. They have remained popular for reasons other than those they might have wished: mainly because of their commendable lyricism and their narrative ability. Pound of course has become by far the greatest poet of them all, having outworn the rather thin delicacy of Imagism a year or two after it attracted him and become the greatest virtuoso poet in the world; but still there is nothing national about his poetry; he derives from and alludes to the literature of the world in his masterpiece, the *Cantos*, and can only be compared with that other master of language James Joyce.

To find the uniquely American voice of poetry as it continued after the magnificent achievements of Walt Whitman—continued, be it noted, with somewhat less intensity—it is necessary to turn to those poets who were describing the decadence of which the Imagists were merely aware.

The most powerful of these is Robinson Jeffers, son of a clergyman, who was born in Pennsylvania in 1887, educated variously in Switzerland, Leipzig, Pennsylvania and Pasadena, and finally settled with his wife in California.

Jeffers's early poems were lyrical in persuasion, strongly influenced by Shelley, and of no great importance; but with *Tamar and Other Poems*, published in 1924 there is nothing that can be dismissed so unceremoniously, for in the title poem there is every evidence of a major poetic mind at work. There is a perfectly reasonable comparison to be made between Jeffers and Eugene O'Neill: both the poet and the dramatist deal with huge, elemental subjects and primitive passions, and both carve their themes massively and without any consideration for the possible consequences of unpopularity; but, even more aptly, they both see with equal clarity the workings of decadence. Jeffers certainly is constantly aware of mankind's urge to self-destruction:

> While this America settles in the
> mould of its vulgarity,
> heavily thickening to empire,

And protest, only a bubble in the
    molten mass, pops and sighs
    out, and the mass hardens,

I sadly smiling remember that
    the flower fades to make fruit,
    the fruit rots to make earth.

And of man's sins of introversion:

Man, introverted man, having crossed
In passage and but a little with the
    nature of things this latter century
Has begot giants; but being taken up
Like a maniac with self-love and
    inward conflicts
    cannot manage his hybrids.

Being used to deal with edgeless dreams
Now he's bred knives on nature, turns
    them also inward:
They have thirsty points though.
His mind forebodes his own destruction.

It is in the introverted mind of humanity that Jeffers finds the motivation for his two greatest works, *Tamar* and *Roan Stallion*. Although rape, murder, suicide and lust all form part of the fabric of these two long narrative poems, it is the unnatural crimes of incest and bestiality (both products of introversion) that concern the poet in his exemplary description of decadence; and it surely can be no coincidence that we find not only the greatest poet and the greatest playwright of America in the twentieth century, but also the greatest novelist too—as will be seen in the section on William Faulkner in the next chapter—all turning to the same basic sin that formed the subject of Sophocles' and Æschylus' interpretation of the decline of Greek civilization, when they seek to interpret present day decadence.

Tamar Cauldwell, a female incarnation of evil whose intense love of sin is expressed in the words 'we must keep sin pure or it will poison us. The grain of goodness in a sin is poison' is to her joy thrown into an incestuous relationship with her brother Lee while she is nursing him after an accident. Pregnant by him she seduces her normal lover Will Andrews so that she can pretend the child is his. Then, learning from the brooding aunt, who is her only protector, that the family history is tainted with the sin of incest, she attempts to procure an abortion. This she does in a strange tribal dance. Then her father curses Lee Cauldwell and Tamar swears revenge on him by seducing him to be her third lover. She finally conceives a plan to set father, lover and brother against one another in a fight of her causing; but she is too enmeshed in their lives to escape punishment (in any case none of the sinners in Jeffers's poems ever goes unpunished) and all four meet their deaths in the flames of a fire begun by Tamar's idiot sister, Jinny.

In *Roan Stallion* Jeffers has taken as a basis of his tale two themes: the Greek myth of Leda and the Swan, and a story attaching to a Turin statue of a horse who took a woman for a lover. It is a tale more Western than the most wild of 'wild west' films, set in Jeffers's adopted territory of California, in which the central character is a beautiful half-breed girl of noble lineage on her mother's side. The girl, who is called California, is married to a wastrel husband called Johnny and has a daughter, Christine. California begins to hate Johnny when he comes home drunk, leading the stallion he has acquired in payment of a gambling debt, having forgotten that it is Christmas and that he should have brought presents for Christine. The stallion is at first the additional object of California's hate, but when in the spring she sees him mated with a mare, she finds her thoughts turning inward to contemplate the stallion's magnificence and her own urgent desire. There is a marvellously described wild ride in which woman and beast are *in communicado* symbolically if not factually, and a resultant loathing for Johnny from whom she flies in horror when he returns. Johnny pursues her with the dog and California traps him into entering the corral where the stallion turns on him and pounds him to death while California shoots the dog and, subsequently, the stallion—though her motive for this last is not understood by her and can only be attributed to 'some obscure human fidelity.' She watches the beautiful stallion fall to the earth with the feelings of a woman 'who has killed God.'

Jeffers's use of these stories of violence and brutality is always cathartic in the Greek sense. Like Sophocles and Æschylus, he uses elements of hatred and torture to show the ultimate deathlessness of the human spirit, never for the sake of glorying in morbidity. The usual denigration of Jeffers's stature as a poet is based on the theory that such wildly sinful people as Tamar and California have no counterparts in ordinary social life and that such violent happenings as they are involved in are incredible. There is a sound basis for such reasoning—which, incidentally, can be equally well applied to *Titus Andronicus, The Jew of Malta* and the Theban plays of Sophocles—but the point that is missed is Jeffers's deliberate elevation of sin to proportions that do not appear puny against the cosmic setting of the California he has chosen. There is a revolutionary vastness about the Pacific coast of America and Jeffers continually apprises his readers of it and of his own awe in its presence:

here the
Pacific—
Our ships, planes, wars are
perfectly irrelevant.
Neither our present blood-feud
with the brave dwarfs

Nor any future world-quarrel
    of westering
And eastering man, the bloody
    migrations, greed of power,
    clash of faiths—
Is a speck of dust on the great
    scale-pan.

Here from this mountain shore,
    headland and beyond stormy
    headland plunging like
    dolphins through the blue
    sea-smoke
Into pale sea—look west at
    the hill of water: it is
    half the planet: this dome,
    this half-globe, this bulging
Eyeball of water, arched over to Asia,

Australia and white Antarctica:
    those are the eyelids
    that never close; this is
    the staring unsleeping
Eye of the earth; and what it
    watches is not our wars.

It is in an effort to show the smallness of sin that Jeffers has raised it to such satanic stature, for at least one can now see it in relation to the cosmic forces and smile at its insignificance, whereas if it had been left in a natural and acceptable magnitude it would have been invisible. But small as sin is, insignificant in relation to the universe, it is none the less man's own downfall and is already destined to bring about his extinction.

Jeffers's uniqueness as an American poet lies in his own apprehension of the nation's particular introversion, 'the mould of its vulgarity,' and its superb vastness as examplified in the Californian scene. In *The Tower Beyond Tragedy* he suggests that man's only hope in his brief span is to live by an extraverted love that has nothing to do with narcissism but is concerned only with geological and cosmic things; it is a pointer to spiritual health that is peculiarly applicable to America.

Of late years poetry in America has become narrower in thematic range and more meticulous in its craftsmanship. The work of poets like Marianne Moore, Archibald MacLeish, E. E. Cummings, William Carlos Williams, Robert Penn Warren, Wallace Stevens and Karl Shapiro is often remarkable for the brilliance of its technique and for characteristically American humour—usually satirical (*cf.* E. E. Cummings); but its main fault as poetry lies in its tendency to be cerebral when dealing with lofty themes and sentimental in its emotional contexts. This is of course a reflexion of the fetish for scholarship that is little more than an attitude to conceal a hollowness in the heart of a great but frantically bewildered nation. Attitudes and fetishes are likely to become apparent in poetry rather sooner than in other forms of literary art.

CHAPTER EIGHT

The Perceptive Few and the Lost Generation

I

WRITERS of the first thirty years of the twentieth century were in the main, as has been seen, concerned with interpreting the disintegrating forces that were propelling human existence forward at an ever-increasing pace. Such an impetus was best recorded by naturalistic and realistic methods that had little or no connexion with classical art forms. The sprawling novels of Dreiser and of another veritable Hindenburg, Thomas Wolfe, can hardly be said to be artistic creations; the tales of Sherwood Anderson, though shapely in feeling are often flat in a constructive sense; the satires of Sinclair Lewis, though excellent in the fulfilment of their ironical purpose, are full of so-called 'characters' who are never realized as people but remain mouthpieces of various viewpoints; the phoney classico-romanticism of Cabell is not much more than an ineffective ball shied at the Aunt Sally of naturalism. Of the writers who bothered less about the pace of living and more about the form in which they should realize it artistically, both T. S. Eliot and Henry James forsook America and found in Europe an environment more suitable for their interpretations. So that the literary history of America was being formed in the main during the first quarter of the twentieth century by writers whose burning interest was in the theme presented rather than the manner of its presentation. But there were two notable exceptions—writers whose concern was equally for the technically artistic shape of the matter presented and whose contributions to American literature, though perhaps not of direct vital importance, were influential in perpetuating technical standards that might otherwise have faded from the ken of the writers of today.

Of these, Edith Wharton has achieved some fame outside America largely because she is a writer who chooses her *locale* from among the cities of Europe rather than her native New York. In this she is like her friend and mentor Henry James, for she was always a European in feeling, had spent much of her childhood there and was to live in France from 1907 until her death in 1937. But still there is far more of the taste of America in her novels than in those of Henry James. In *The Age of Innocence*, for example, which won the Pulitzer Prize in 1920, she gives a remarkably realistic picture of the New York of the post-Civil War period and treats the social conventions of the time with perceptive irony; and in *The Custom of the Country* she is concerned with French and American marriages and the contrast between them, and once again treats her theme with disillusioned irony.

Edith Wharton had been writing all her life: even in her childhood she was sending poems to Longfellow, who passed them on to *The Atlantic Monthly*—which, incidentally, printed them—and she never failed to construct her novels with every emphasis on the artistic form. She hated the shapeless methods of the English biographical novel that sprawled loosely over endless issues of a magazine and she could see no joy in the creation of a character unless that character could be fitted with artistic perfection into the whole. The theme that she treated best was that depicting a single character at variance with a social group, the conflict between individual and group being usually motivated by the taboos and favoured customs of the leisured class.

In *Ethan Frome* the background is an agrarian one with

no sign of the glittering drawing-room of Paris or New York; but the awareness of taboos is as strong as ever, and in a story that is as austere as the Starkfield of its *locale*. Edith Wharton raises to almost noble stature a theme that, treated without a fastidious awareness of artistic form, would have been simply a cheap novelette.

Ethan Frome is in fact a novelette in length, but there any implication of tawdriness must end. The outline of the story is simple enough: Ethan Frome, a New England farmer, has been trapped into marrying a quite unsuitable wife (here the conventions of the countryside can be seen through Edith Wharton's customary bitter irony), and because of his unhappiness is more susceptible to the love of the servant girl Mattie Silver. There is no escape for them, for they have no money to run away, and the thought of the clandestine affair they must carry on under the wife's nose is repulsive to them. Thus they are driven to plan a suicide pact. But death evades them and they are left to suffer the working out of a tragedy that achieves terrifying dimensions. The book is to a certain extent damaged artistically by a contrivance of twist endings that might have been supplied by that inveterate twister William Sidney Porter; but elsewhere the construction is superb. From the opening pages:

> I had the story bit by bit, from various people, and, as generally happens in such cases, each time it was a different story.
>
> If you know Starkfield, Massachusetts, you know the post-office. If you know the post-office you must have seen Ethan Frome drive up to it, drop the reins on his hollow-backed bay and drag himself across the brick pavement to the white colonnade: and you must have asked who he was.
>
> It was there that, several years ago, I saw him for the first time; and the sight pulled me up sharp. Even then he was the most striking figure in Starkfield, though he was but the ruin of a man. It was not so much his great height that marked him, for the 'natives' were easily singled out by their lank longitude from the stockier foreign breed: it was the

careless powerful look he had, in spite of a lameness checking each step like the jerk of a chain. There was something bleak and unapproachable in his face, and he was so stiffened and grizzled that I took him for an old man and was surprised to hear that he was not more than fifty-two. I had this from Harmon Gow, who had driven the stage from Bettisbridge to Starkfield in pre-trolley days and knew the chronicle of all the families on his line.

'He's looked that way ever since he had his smash-up; and that's twenty-four years ago come next February,' Harmon threw out between reminiscent pauses.

The 'smash-up' it was—I gathered from the same informant—which, besides drawing the red gash across Ethan Frome's forehead, had so shortened and warped his right side that it cost him a visible effort to take the few steps from his buggy to the post-office window. He used to drive in from his farm every day at about noon, and as that was my own hour for fetching my mail I often passed him in the porch or stood beside him while we waited on the motions of the distributing hand behind the grating. I noticed that, though he came so punctually, he seldom received anything but a copy of the *Bettisbridge Eagle*, which he put without a glance into his sagging pocket. At intervals, however, the postmaster would hand him an envelope addressed to Mrs Zenobia —or Mrs Zeena—Frome, and usually bearing conspiciously in the upper left-hand corner the address of some manufacturer of patent medicine and the name of his specific. These documents my neighbour would also pocket without a glance, as if too much used to them to wonder at their number and variety, and would then turn away with a silent nod to the postmaster.

Every one in Starkfield knew him and gave him a greeting tempered to his own grave mien; but his taciturnity was respected and it was only on rare occasions that one of the older men of the place detained him for a word. When this happened he would listen quietly, his blue eyes on the speaker's face, and answer in so low a tone that his words never reached me; then he would climb stiffly into his buggy, gather up the reins in his left hand and drive slowly away in the direction of his farm.

'It was a pretty bad smash-up?' I questioned Harmon, looking after Frome's retreating figure, and thinking how gallantly his lean brown head, with his shock of light hair, must have sat on his strong shoulders before they were bent out of shape.

'Wust kind,' my informant assented. 'More'n enough to kill most men. But the Fromes are tough. Ethan'll likely touch a hundred.'

'Good God!' I exclaimed. At the moment Ethan Frome, after climbing

> to his seat, had leaned over to assure himself of the security of a wooden box—also with a druggist's label on it—which he had placed in the back of the buggy, and I saw his face as it probably looked when he thought himself alone. '*That* man touch a hundred? He looks as if he was dead and in hell now!'

The story gathers momentum in a magnificent sweep until the close nine short chapters later; and Edith Wharton puts no foot wrong until the dubious ending. It is a *tour de force* of *conte* length, French in the simplicity of its outline but with undertones that are nothing if not American.

This disciplined style is the basis not only of *Ethan Frome* but of all Edith Wharton's novels and stories. It is a style ideally suited to the exploration of themes of ironic cruelty. The complete refinement of her method of delineating the tortures of social conventions has a shattering effect on the nerves of a sensitive reader, who, seeing that Edith Wharton is really a naturalistic writer at heart, perceives, as the author fully intended, that the upper strata of society are not without their social tragedies and that squalor inhabits the social register as well as the gutter.

Edith Wharton has had a number of followers who have helped to perpetuate her subtle criticism of social life, the most important of them being John P. Marquand, who writes long best-selling novels of a particularly American authenticity in which the moral laws of the Puritans' descendants are set down as barricades against the happiness of the individuals who uphold them.

The tradition of refinement perpetuated from Edith Wharton, William Dean Howells and Henry James, by writers of the technical assurance of Marquand, is perhaps as near as can be got to an Austen quality of wit in America; but it is a tradition of marked importance in a literature that has become overweighted with naturalism of the more sombre order.

Any reference to the changing aspect of American

literature—the change characterized by the shift from nineteenth-century Romanticism to twentieth-century Naturalism—would be incomplete without some notice of Willa Cather, who is important because, in addition to being concerned, like Sarah Orne Jewett, with the internal weakening of Romanticism, she re-established metaphysical values in a corpus of fiction that had been too long without them, and thus forms a convenient link between the earlier naturalistic writers—Crane, Norris, London—and William Faulkner, who also is deeply concerned with mankind's relationship to the ultimate problems.

Willa Sibert Cather was born in Virginia in 1876, but moved to Nebraska with her parents while she was still a child. The prairie environment of the West made a great impression on her, and although she took up journalism and worked for a time in New York as editor of *McClure's Magazine*, it was the regional appeal of that vast western land that filled most of her novels. *My Antonia*, *O, Pioneers!* and *A Lost Lady* are her best works in this genre and in all three of them the outstanding qualities are her sensitivity in the matter of local colour, her perfect fusion of the characteristics of land and people, and her ready perception of the importance of environment on character.

Antonia Shimerda of *My Antonia* is useless in the town, her character is weakened and she begins to disintegrate; yet as soon as she returns to the prairie her natural vitality emerges once more and her stature as a human being is regained. Marian Forrester in *A Lost Lady* is the subject of another study of environment, this time of environment having the opposite effect: for she is a girl who lacks the endurance necessary for the life of austere beauty the prairie offers and she quickly falls from the state of native grace typified by her railway-engineer husband and becomes a bawdy good-time girl whose tragedy is the greater because acted out in a time of transition. No one is more adept at objectively describing the processes of change than Willa Cather. She is neither reactionary nor progressive to a fanatical degree, but she sees clearly enough—and rightly—that it is impossible to maintain accustomed degrees of dignity and nobility in an era that is becoming remarkable only for shrewdness and materialism.

Although not adventurous in the sense of active excitements, all Willa Cather's works deals with adventures of the spirit. In *The Song of the Lark* she tells the story of a Colorado village girl who becomes a prima donna, travels and develops into a sophisticated artist, but narrows rather than widens her experience of life as a consequence of her sophistication. The theme of a painter or musician developing in a world of *bourgeois* values is a favourite one with Willa Cather. It is treated with exquisite irony several times in the collection of short stories *Youth and the Bright Medusa*, wherein lie several of the author's most stylistically polished pieces. The opening of *A Gold Slipper* is a good example of the apparently artless style that on analysis is seen to be rhythmically perfect and delicately tinged with irony:

> Marshall McKann followed his wife and her friend Mrs Post down the aisle and up the steps to the stage of the Carnegie Music Hall with an ill-concealed feeling of grievance. Heaven knew he never went to concerts, and to be mounted upon the stage in this fashion, as if he were a 'highbrow' from Sewickley, or some unfortunate with a musical wife, was ludicrous. A man went to concerts when he was courting, while he was a junior partner. When he became a person of substance he stopped that sort of nonsense. His wife, too, was a sensible person, the daughter of an old Pittsburg family as solid and well-rooted as the McKanns. She would never have bothered about this concert had not the meddlesome Mrs Post arrived to pay her a visit. Mrs Post was an old school friend of Mrs McKann, and because she lived in Cincinnati she was always keeping up with the world and talking about things in which no one else was interested, music among them. She was an aggressive lady, with weighty opinions, and a deep voice like a jovial bassoon. She had arrived only last night, and at dinner she had

brought it out that she could on no account miss Kitty Ayrshire's recital; it was, she said, the sort of thing no one could afford to miss.

In the two historical novels *Death Comes for the Archbishop* and *Shadows on the Rock* there is a considerable loss of technical tension because of the loose episodic construction; but this is fully compensated for by the spiritual intensity of the atmosphere of the past that pervades both books. In both stories the Church is the mediating influence between man and his eternal problems. This affirmation of metaphysical values that had become lost in the swirl of naturalism, agnosticism and heresy is a gentle reminder from an artist of considerable talent that although a realistic approach to life has its merits there is an enduring satisfaction to be found in the stories of men and women who maintain positive standards of courage and honesty in the face of enveloping materialism—even though those men and women may be quite unaware of their inherent idealism.

Willa Cather's work, though lacking the positive strength that might have raised her to the stature of Whitman, has its own importance in the literature of America: it is an importance somewhat akin to that of Mark Twain's, though no one would claim for her that she had the same narrative ability or picaresque humour. She has skilfully deduced, as did Mark Twain, a universal significance from a parochial setting, and every single one of her characters, whether delineated in two paragraphs or two hundred pages, is a human being, clearly individualized and indubitably American.

II

In 1949 the Nobel Prize for literature was awarded to William Faulkner, a novelist whose power had been recognized twenty years previously by Arnold Bennett, who spoke of him as writing 'like an angel,' and by many other perceptive critics in England and France, but whose sales in America had remained steadily, like Gertrude Stein's, at the two-thousand-copies-a-book level. On accepting the prize from the King of Sweden in Stockholm Faulkner said this:

> I feel that this award was not made to me as a man but to my work—a life's work in the agony and sweat of the human spirit, not for glory and least of all for profit, but to create out of the materials of the human spirit something which did not exist before. So this award is only mine in trust. It will not be difficult to find a dedication for the money part of it commensurate with the purpose and significance of its origin. But I would like to do the same with the acclaim too, by using this moment as a pinnacle from which I might be listened to by the young men and women already dedicated to the same anguish and travail, among whom is already standing that one who will some day stand here where I am standing.
>
> Our tragedy today is a general and universal physical fear so long sustained by now that we can even bear it. There are no longer problems of the spirit. There is only the question: When will I be blown up? Because of this, the young man or woman writing today has forgotten the problems of the human heart in conflict with itself which alone can make good writing because only that is worth writing about, worth the agony and the sweat.
>
> He must learn them again. He must teach himself that the basest of all things is to be afraid; and, teaching himself that, forget it forever, leaving no room in his workshop for anything but the old verities and truths of the heart, the old universal truths without which any story is ephemeral and doomed—love and honour and pity and pride and compassion and sacrifice. Until he does so, he labours under a curse. He writes not of love but of lust, of defeats in which nobody loses anything of value, of victories without hope and, worst of all, without pity and compassion. His griefs grieve on no universal bones, leaving no scars. He writes not of the heart but of the glands.
>
> Until he relearns these things, he will write as though he stood alone and watched the end of man. I decline to accept the end of man. It is easy enough to say that man is immortal because he will endure; that when the last ding-dong of doom has changed and faded from the last red and dying evening, that even then there will be one more sound: that of his puny inexhaustible voice, still talking. I refuse to accept this.

believe that man will not merely endure: he will prevail. He is immortal, not because he alone among creatures has an inexhaustible voice but because he has a soul, a spirit capable of compassion and sacrifice and endurance. The poet's, the writer's, duty is to write about these things. It is his privilege to help man endure by lifting his heart, by reminding him of the courage and honour and hope and pride and compassion and pity and sacrifice which have been the glory of his past. The poet's voice need not merely be the record of man, it can be one of the props, the pillars to help him endure and prevail.

This may seem to the ordinary reader, knowing only the name and nothing of the work of Faulkner, to be a rhetorical speech for a rhetorical occasion. He will note the basic simplicity of the phrasing and its deliberate elaboration by euphony, ornament and repetition, and will perhaps conclude that here certainly is a piece suitable for inclusion in future anthologies of American prose—a conclusion fully justified and doubtless to be proved correct. But he is mistaken if he assumes that it is a special occasional piece that bears no relation to the rest of Faulkner's work; for it is typical, both in style and content, of the Mississippi novelist's entire output. The technical virtuoso who can if he wishes write as simply as this—

He came up the drive and stopped before the house, where his grandfather sat with his feet on the veranda railing and Miss Jenny stood trim in her black dress beside a post (*Sartoris*)

can also write as elaborately as this—

He was not escaping it; symbolic and encompassing, it outlay all gasoline-spanned distances and all clock- or sun-stipulated destinations It would be there—the eternal swell of the coffee the sugar the hemp sweating slow iron plates above the forked deliberate brown water and lost all ultimate blue of latitude and horizon; the hot rain gutterful plaiting the eaten heads of shrimp; the ten thousand inescapable mornings wherein ten thousand swinging airplants stippleprop the soft scrofulous soaring of sweating brick and ten thousand pairs of splayed brown hired Leonora feet tiger-baned by jaloused armistice with the invincible sun: the thin black coffee, the myriad oil—tomorrow and tomorrow and tomorrow; not only to hope, not even to wait: just to endure (*Pylon*).

And it must be said at the outset of any introduction to his work that the incessant monstrous over-writing and nonsensical syntax (not to mention the frequent appalling grammar and peculiar spelling) cannot by any means be considered apart from the work itself. They are not to be defended or attacked or to have 'allowances' made for them. For it can now be seen—after more than twenty books—that the technical methods *are* the work and quite inseparable from any consideration of theme or character. It is also now apparent that it is difficult to make any critical assessment of individual books in the saga of the South that is Faulkner's life work as a writer—and this in spite of the fact that the saga is still incomplete. But it is at least possible —and necessary—to survey the work and try to place it in relation to American literature as a whole.

Faulkner was born in New Albany, Mississippi, in 1897, his father being a business manager of the University there. He had at least one literary antecedent in his great-grandfather, William C. Faulkner, an author of sentimental romantic novels of the kind that are still world best sellers, though today they seem to be written by Mrs Frances Parkinson Keyes. As a child he moved to the town of Oxford, also in Mississippi, and apart from his First World War service with the Royal Flying Corps and a brief stay with Sherwood Anderson in New Orleans has lived there ever since, in the colonial-type house of his aristocratic ancestors.

So far as his saga of the south is concerned Faulkner has limited the geographical aspect of his study to some 2000 square miles of land north of the Mississippi hills and called by him Yoknapatawpha County. The capital town he calls Jefferson. It is as well to be clear at the start that Faulkner is actually writing about Oxford, the town in which he lives, which is in fact the capital of Lafayette County, Mississippi (only the State has remained without a pseudonym in his invention). All but two of his books are concerned wholly or for the main part with the people of Yoknapatawpha County. The exceptions are *Mosquitoes* and *Pylon*, both of which are set in New Orleans. In the Yoknapatawpha County books Faulkner follows the fortunes of various families—the Sutpens, the Compsons, the Snopeses, the Benbows, the Bundrens, the Sartorises—who are representative of various social strata; but he doesn't necessarily follow them chronologically or even manage to remain consistent in his details, so that minor (but never major) characters are liable to crop up in different books with different Christian names or different complexions or different hair; nor does he find it necessary to eschew experiment for the sake of consistency in the whole (*Light of August* has a shape that necessitates beginning the story at the beginning; *Absalom! Absalom!* has a shape into which entry can be made, as into *Finnegans Wake*, at any point); all of which makes it a little difficult for the reader, who is liable to be foxed as much by some inconsequential inconsistency as by the frequent tortuousness of Faulkner's narrative.

The subjects chosen by Faulkner are just as violent, and rather more varied, than those chosen by Robinson Jeffers. Incest, rape, miscegenation, murder, imbecility—they are all in the Yoknapatawpha saga in the fullest of full strengths. But the blessing of humour is mercifully added to ease the fascinated reader's sombre burden. Ingenuity of plot too: *Smoke* is a bit of logical detection worthy of every principle of Poe. So that one way and another the reader can get along if he can only delay his impatience as to what the saga is about until he has read at least eight of the Yoknapatawpha books. By that time the pattern will begin to emerge.

The ostensible theme of the whole saga is the degeneracy of the South. Shrewdness and greed (represented by the upstart Snopes family) are shown as overcoming the honest traditions of the aristocratic Sartorises; but at the same time the internal weakness of the ancient Southerners is shown to be a result of their own shrewdness and greed back in the early days of colonization when they wrested land from the Indian population and put the Negroes in bondage. But the evolutionary spiral is in fact symbolic of fear more than of the destruction of the deep South; like Melville, Faulkner clearly shows his intention of symbolizing inter-racial conflict, for his Yoknapatawpha is a minescule world with Memphis as the Vanity Fair in which all the rather ghastly pleasure seeking is done, and his characters imply far more than dialectal differences.

If one is to attempt to seek a single Faulkner book in which the decadence of the South (and implicitly of the world) is explored more or less completely between two covers, without too much reference to what has happened in previous books and what is about to happen in later ones, and in which too intense an effort of imagination and concentration is not required of the reader, the goal is to be found more readily in *Light of August* than in any other of Faulkner's novels. Also this book makes a good introduction to Faulkner on the grounds that, though not so carefully constructed as *Absalom! Absalom!* (his finest novel from a technical viewpoint) it is far easier to read.

Light in August tells two stories: the first about a village girl's search for the father of her child, the second about the persecution of a foundling boy, Joe Christmas. The method employed is very Conradian in its mirror-within-mirror technique. From the opening pages, in which Lena Grove is seen waiting for a wagon to take her on to the next village to continue her search for the lover who has deserted her, the two parallel stories penetrate further and further into the heart of the book and then gradually emerge again after involving the reader in the murder of Miss Burden by Joe Christmas, the horrifying lynching of Christmas by Percy Grimm, and the birth of Lena Grove's baby. The word 'involving' is used deliberately, for Faulkner has the power to force his reader to participate in the events of his stories—a power that he shares with Hawthorne. Any consideration of this power must involve a consideration of the difficulties of reading Faulkner, for it now emerges clearly that his ratiocinative (it is one of his own favourite words) sentences are not altogether wilfully obfusc, but are intended so to capture the reader's attention that his participation in the events of the books, and his realization that he too is responsible for his share in their outcome, are inevitable.

Faulkner's publishers refer to his style as 'tightly coiled' and if one reads the following single sentence from *Intruder in the Dust* one sees all too clearly what they mean:

> Nor one school-bound child on the street although he had heard without listening enough of his uncle at the telephone to know that the superintendent had called whether to have school today or not and his uncle had told him yes, and in sight of the Square now he could see already three more of the yellow busses supposed and intended to bring the county children into school but which their owner-contractor-operators translated on Saturdays and holidays into pay-passenger transport and then the Square itself, the parked cars and trucks as always as should be but the Square itself anything but empty: no exodus of men toward the stock pens nor women into the stores so that as he drove the pickup into the kerb behind his uncle's car he could see already where visible and sense where not a moil and mass of movement, one dense pulse and hum filling the Square as when the crowd overflows the carnival midway or the football field, flowing into the street and already massed along the opposite side to the jail until the head of it had already passed the blacksmith's where he had stood yesterday trying to be invisible as if they were waiting for a parade to pass (and almost in the middle of the street so that the still unbroken stream of cars and trucks had to detour around them a clump of a dozen or so more like the group in a reviewing stand in whose centre in its turn

he recognized the badged official cap of the town marshal who at this hour on this day would have been in front of the schoolhouse holding up traffic for children to cross the street and he did not have to remember that the marshal's name was Ingrum, a Beat Four Ingrum come to town as the apostate sons of Beat Four occasionally did to marry a town girl and become barbers and bailiffs and night-watchmen as pretty Germanic princelings would come down out of their Brandenburg hills to marry the heiresses to European thrones)—the men and the women and not one child, the weathered country faces and sunburned necks and backs of hands, the clean faded tieless earth-coloured shirts and pants and print-coloured dresses thronging the Square and the street as though the stores themselves were closed and locked, not even staring at the blank front of the jail and the single barred window which had been empty and silent too for going on forty-eight hours now but just gathering, condensing, not expectant nor in anticipation nor even attentive yet but merely in that preliminary settling down like the before-curtain in a theatre: and he thought that was it: holiday: which meant a day for children yet here turned upside down: and suddenly he realized that he had been completely wrong; it was not Saturday which had never happened but only last night which to them had not happened yet, that not only they didn't know about last night but there was nobody, not even Hampton, who could have told them because they would have refused to believe him; whereupon something like a skin or a veil like that which crosses a chicken's eye and which he had not even known was there went flick! from his own and he saw them for the first time—the same weathered still almost inattentive faces and the same faded clean cotton shirts and pants and dresses but no crowd now waiting for the curtain to rise on a stage's illusion but rather the one in the courtroom waiting for the sheriff's officer to cry Oyez Oyez Oyez This honourable court; not even impatient because the moment had not even come yet to sit in judgment not on Lucas Beauchamp, they had already condemned him but on Beat Four, come not to see what they called justice done nor even retribution exacted but to see that Beat Four should not fail its white man's high estate.

Intruder in the Dust marks an important shift in moral emphasis in Faulkner's work. Hitherto his books have been concerned with the dominance of evil, misanthropy and humour of the grim variety, although always there is at least one hopeful or happy character—even though that character's happiness may be due to ignorance or insanity.

But with *Intruder in the Dust*, published in 1949, the dominance of justice is an assumed thing—in spite of the fact that it is a Negro who has to be proved innocent of the murder of the white man.

With Faulkner as with James Joyce the reader's complete immolation is demanded—not merely to the book that is engaging his immediate attention but to the complete saga of Southern decadence that the author has painted slowly and painfully over the years since 1926. The reader must be astute in his perception of the extensive genealogy of the Compsons, the Sutpens, the Snopeses and the rest, and must also have a view of the delta country around Jackson, Mississippi, in his mind's eye. These last are not so difficult as may appear, for there are clues in every book; nor is the 'tightly coiled' style so formidable when once the reader acquires the knack of coping with it, for invariably the elongated sentences are the ones used simply to build up the elaborate atmosphere of psychological complication, while the machinations of the plot are much more simply stated—often in dialogue or brief sentences packed with action:

> While on his way to Pensacola to visit his mother, Popeye was arrested in Birmingham for the murder of a policeman in a small Alabama town on June 17 of that year. It was on the night of June 17 that Temple had passed him sitting in the parked car beside the road house on the night when Red had been killed. Each summer Popeye went to see his mother. She thought he was a night clerk in a Memphis hotel.
>
> His mother was the daughter of a boarding-house keeper. His father had been a professional strike-breaker hired by the street railway company to break a strike in 1900. His mother at that time was working in a department store down-town. For three nights she rode home on the car beside the motorman's seat on which Popeye's father rode. One night the strike-breaker got off at the corner with her and walked to her home.
>
> 'Won't you get fired?' she said.
>
> 'By who?' the strike-breaker said. They walked along together. He

was well dressed. 'Them others would take me that quick. They know it too.'

'Who would take you?'

'The strikers. I don't care a damn who is running the car, see. I'll ride with one as soon as another. Sooner, if I could make this route every night at this time.'

She walked beside him. 'You don't mean that,' she said.

'Sure I do.' He took her arm.

'I guess you'd just as soon be married to one as another, the same way.'

'Who told you that?' he said. 'Have them bastards been talking about me?'

A month later she told him they would have to be married.

'How do you mean, have to?' he said.

'I don't dare to tell them. I would have to go away. I don't dare.'

'Well, don't get upset. I'd just as lief. I have to pass here every night, anyway.'

They were married.

The reader who perseveres with the work of this remarkable writer will find himself moved alternately by compassion and despair; he will find humour of grim sophistication and bucolic fancy; and the most powerful awareness of evil since the plays of the Elizabethan dramatists. But it becomes more apparent as time goes on and each new volume is added to the saga that Faulkner is not the chronicler of evil morbidity he was once believed to be: he is aware equally of justice and sentiment, and of the virtues he loves most of all to stress—love, honour, courage, pride and humility. His stature, now that it begins to merge into perspective, is seen clearly to be that of the greatest of all American prose writers of the twentieth century.

III

The South, with its immense potentiality as a symbol of world unrest, is being exploited in literature by a good many writers who, lacking Faulkner's power, are content to work within narrower limits. Of these, Katherine Anne Porter, Carson McCullers and Eudora Welty are noteworthy examples among the women, Erskine Caldwell among the men. All three concern themselves with a multiplicity of psychological detail in preference to essentials, so that often their stories gain in atmosphere only at the expense of strength. Like those intensely nervous people who concentrate on every aspect of planning a journey except the important one of catching the train, they tend to be introspective and sensitive in the extreme.

Katherine Anne Porter is the most intellectually mature of the three. Her style is simple and straightforward and has something of Edith Wharton's ironic leaning toward the genteel. All her best work is in short-story or *conte* form, and all her thirty or so stories—her entire output—show an intense awareness of the 'desolation of the spirit, the chill and the knowledge of death.'

Carson McCullers is a specialist in the study of solitude. All her characters suffer isolation like a mental illness. Whatever the outward form of their cruelty one to the other they are all concerned knowingly or unknowingly with the pursuit of something that is much too complex to be called simply happiness. There is no atmosphere of blank misery in her stories, but a delicate and poignant yearning for the indefinable haunts everything and everyone in them.

Eudora Welty too specializes in lonely and humbled people whom she invests with an immense human dignity. But though dignified in conception her characters are sometimes robbed of that dignity by their author's execution of them. For her style is often ridden with superfluous whimsicalities, quaint names and charming but irrelevant images. She is a regionalist writer whose themes are invariably universal in their appeal but who tends to become wearying because of her mannered style of writing. The power of her poetic imagination is, however, very great; and her most remarkable successes occur in those stories such as *The Wide Net* and *The Robber Bridegroom* in which she combines the elements of fantasy and reality.

Erskine Caldwell has investigated one particular aspect of Southern poverty with great effect and considerable repetition. It is the premise made clear in his first important book *Tobacco Road* (subsequently filmed and staged with great success)—the premise that in the sharecropper's grim life there is not, and never can be, any joys but the sensual ones of sex. Most of his short stories are directed toward the same end. But with *Trouble in July*, published in 1940, he turns from the earthy humours of the Lester family in *Tobacco Road* to draw up one of the most powerful indictments against racial discrimination ever written.

Trouble in July is about a lynching, but instead of soliciting the reader's sympathy for the victim Caldwell penetrates with blistering insight into the psychology of mass hypnosis. There are moments of horror in this story greater even than the capture of Joe Christmas in Faulkner's *Light in August*; and an extreme irony is added by having the tale narrated by the sheriff, whose only real concern is to get himself away from the scene of the trouble he knows is boiling up all too fast in his Georgia town.

Caldwell is a writer of limited range but great power and the influence of his style has been considerable—particularly on the Raymond Chandler and James M. Cain schools of thriller writers, who have added an urban sophistication to naturalistic themes that derive, via Caldwell and Garland, from Zola and the other European exponents of naturalism.

IV

The extensive subject-matter of Walt Whitman's poetry, the hugely compassionate interest that made him want to include everything and everybody pertaining to America in his poems, is the ideal aimed at in prose by John Dos Passos, the Chicago novelist, born in 1896. The ideal came closest to attainment in the massive trilogy of his novels generically entitled *U.S.A.* published between 1930 and 1936. The three novels, *The 42nd Parallel*, *1919* and *The Big Money* cover the period 1910–35 and follow the life stories of ten principal characters. These characters are set in a colossal photographic background made up of thousands of miniature scenes, scraps of dialogue, 'camera-eye' impressions, journalistic reports, noises off, and every possible device that can be brought in to aid the impression of completeness. And there is no doubt that the impression has been created. The reader feels quite convinced that what he is looking at is a kind of super-Dickensian picture of America, immense with the diversity of its humanity and the teeming life of its cities. This impression is often so strong as to be astounding; the reader almost has to pinch himself to take his eyes from the vast canvas so that he can turn to look out of his own window and put himself back on the realistic footing of real life and confirm that what he sees through his own window is precisely what Dos Passos has just been showing him.

But if he begins to think hard enough and goes on thinking long enough, he will begin to see that something is actually missing from Dos Passos' canvas: there is background and foreground but no middle distance in the picture; it is so full of event and action that no room at all has been left for the millions of ordinary people whose lives are a daily commuting linking the cradle and the grave; the events and action concern exclusively the 'workers' and the 'capitalists.' This is not meant to imply that Don Passos is a Marxist writer whose sympathies are with the revolutionary school and who dreams of the day when the gutters will run with the blood of the *petit bourgeousie*. Nothing could be further from the truth. His sympathies certainly lie with the underdog, and the tycoon J. W. Moorehouse in *U.S.A.* is shown as dangerous in the sense that he sells ideas that many people come to look upon as ideals; but Dos Passos' failure to establish a middle distance, a norm that can be sounded as a basic keynote to which the reader has continual reference, is not due to any proletarian intentions. It appears to be primarily due to an artistic failure in Dos Passos himself—a failure of the imagination that can conceive high drama only in terms of extremes, never in terms of the simple dreariness of which so many millions' lives consist, in America as elsewhere.

This, then, means that *U.S.A.* is not truly representative as a picture of America, in spite of the enormous technical skill that has gone to its construction. But this would not matter if there were not another more important failure in the whole conception. This lies in a certain tendency for the work—and for Don Passos' fiction as a whole—to demand an almost esoteric knowledge of America for its complete understanding. And a picture that purports to be valuable as art must in some way overcome the barriers of nationality if it is to be successful. Those regionalist writers who have added to the stature of American literature, even though their range is of the very narrowest, e.g. Sarah Orne Jewett and Eudora Welty, have succeeded because their artistic conscience forbade them to deal with themes of any but universal interest. But Don Passos has allowed himself to present America to the Americans instead of to the rest of the world; and his achievement is therefore artistically the less.

But there is no doubt of the importance of his technical

innovations. The apparent trend of his thought, too, was taken far too literally by a good many of the 'proletarian' writers of the between-wars period, notably James T. Farrell, whose Marxian bitterness found its most effective form in another trilogy of Chicago life, *Studs Lonigan*, a study in the boyhood, adolescence and manhood of a character on whom the slum environment of his upbringing has a formative effect. Farrell says of his own creation:

> Studs Lonigan is neither a tough nor a gangster. He is not really a hard guy. He is a normal young American of his time and class. His values become the values of his world. He has as many good impulses as normal human beings have. In time, because of defeat, of frustration, of a total situation characterized by spiritual poverty, these good impulses are expressed more and more in the stream of his reverie. Here we find the source of Studs' constant dream of himself. Studs' dream of himself changes in character as the story progresses. In the beginning, it is a vision of what he is going to be. He is a boy waiting at the threshold of life. His dream of himself is a romantic projection of the future, conceived in the terms and values of his world. In time, this dream of himself turns backward. It is no longer a projection of romantic things to come. More and more it becomes a nostalgic image turned toward the past. Does not this happen in a greater or lesser degree to all of us?

Does it not indeed? But the idea can scarcely be claimed as an original one: it is effective in Farrell's trilogy because he has absorbed many of the technical innovations of Dos Passos and some of the religious prejudices of James Joyce, plus much of the 'street-scene' detail that had become *de rigueur* since Zola and combined them all with the determination to prove that it is environment alone that causes Studs Lonigan's disintegration and death at the age of thirty. The book remains, however, a powerful indictment of poverty and the repressions forced on a decent young man by conventions.

V

When Gertrude Stein referred to the 'lost generation' she meant those writers and artists who appeared to have lost their illusions about life and could portray the world only through their own spiritual disintegration—which they were well aware of but could do nothing to arrest. A writer like Faulkner could interpret decadence and disintegration from the positive standpoint of his own personality without ever implying that he himself was part of that disintegration and decadence; but a writer like F. Scott Fitzgerald was necessarily involved personally. Necessarily, because all his life he had only the fragile illusion of wealth to cling to and there is no illusion that disintegrates more easily.

But Fitzgerald spoke for a million undergraduates and good-timers of the jazz age, and there is scarcely any better chronicle of degeneracy than *The Great Gatsby*, published in 1925. The selfishness of the post-war boom period with its glitter and its harsh and tawdry parties is nowhere better summed up than in the single sentence from the book:

> They were careless people, Tom and Daisy—they smashed up things and creatures and then retreated back into their money or their vast carelessness or whatever it was that kept them together, and let people clean up the mess they had made.

Fitzgerald enjoyed great success in his lifetime and achieved a literary vogue that in perspective is seen to be founded almost solely on *The Great Gatsby*. But he lived to be only forty-four and it is doubtful if, even had he lived longer, he would have been able to reach again the excellence of that book. For the writer who has a belief neither in himself nor in any set of spiritual values is at more of a loss than he, not caring, can know.

The difference between the nihilistic attitude of Fitzgerald and that of Ernest Hemingway in both authors' early writings is difficult to determine. Their subject-matter is easily distinguishable: Fitzgerald is attracted by flappers and undergraduates and wealthy legatees, while Hemingway goes out for much tougher material—stories of backwoodsmen, whores, drunks, race-track types and soldiers. But this thematic difference is irrelevant. It can only be suggested that the essential difference in their attitude to life lies in the fact that Hemingway's nihilism covertly conceals beneath its hard bright cynicism the seed of the positive values in which he was later to demonstrate his faith.

Hemingway is the son of a doctor and was born in Illinois in 1898. His schooldays proved him an excellent sportsman and he has remained one ever since. After his war service with an ambulance unit in Italy he became a foreign correspondent on the *Toronto Star* and later a correspondent for a newspaper syndicate stationed in Paris. There he met Sherwood Anderson and Gertrude Stein and decided on the career of writer.

His first published volume of stories and poems showed the influence of Anderson, Crane and Fitzgerald; the second, *In Our Time*, showed an even more important influence—that of Gertrude Stein. Although Hemingway owes nothing else to Gertrude Stein, it can hardly be denied that the brief, colloquial style that has been imitated by legions of writers is intimately connected with the dissociation-of-words-and-ideas method that she experimented with in her 'automatic' writings. But Hemingway was trying to do something of much more positive value in his experiments: he was trying to clear the decks of literature of all the lumber of simile and image, of adjective and superlative, that it had collected during the decay of Romanticism. He saw the need for an infusion of honesty, of clarity and diamond-hard brilliance to counteract the mush and sentimentality that had accumulated; and his integrity was such that he could not allow himself to exploit anything but the cynical disillusionments he felt about his recent war experiences.

In Hemingway's first novel *Fiesta* appear the first signs of his development toward a set of positive values. In this story, told by an ex-soldier who has been rendered sterile by his war wound, there is a deal of cynicism, but also a deal of genuine suffering which is observable to the reader but not to the characters, who spend much of their time trying to forget situations they haven't the courage to face.

From that time onward, all through the superb reporting and infinite poignancy of *A Farewell to Arms, Death in the Afternoon* and *For Whom the Bell Tolls,* as well as the *contes* and stories (e.g. *The Snows of Kilimanjaro* and *The Short Happy Life of Francis Macomber*) that have attained their place among the masterpieces of world fiction, there has been a gradual affirmation of Hemingway's acquisition of a belief, or set of beliefs. It is not a happy or even a hopeful attitude that he has acquired; the presence of death is a constant factor in his work; but it appears more and more often in his later books that he wishes to underline the significance of loyalty in the human character. Sensuality, toughness, a certain tendency to inverted romanticism —these continue to be his materials, but the extreme vitality of his writing is no longer lost in the mid-air of nihilism.

Hemingway's importance as a writer is undoubted; as a writer concerning himself with specifically American problems he is far less important. Americans people his books and stories, but they are often exiled through the exigencies of war or other circumstances, or, like Hemingway himself, they are great travellers and hunters. He has derived from, and added to, the work of his American predecessors and contemporaries in the field of technique particularly; but he remains a writer unbounded by the frontiers of nationality, as much of England, Spain, France and Africa as of the land of his birth. And his stature is of true greatness.

CHAPTER NINE

The Past and the Future

I

It will now be clearly seen that American literature, having absorbed European influences for some two hundred years, began in the nineteenth century to achieve a lively and distinctive quality of its own. The immense creative forces of the Renaissance and the Reformation were translated by the colonizers from 1492 onward to the newly discovered land of opportunity and were there released without opposition from any existing culture. The civilization of Columbus's 'Indians' was peremptorily dealt with by the simple process of pushing the nomadic outposts of Aztec and Inca culture back beyond the Atlantic coastal mountains where they were out of sight, out of mind, and beyond hearing. And as their culture was almost exclusively oral and pictorial it offered little resistance to a creative spirit that had acquired the disseminative attribute of the craft of printing.

It will be clear too that the manifest genius of the early settlers was for political literature rather than for the literature of entertainment. This naturally arose from the fact that first things must come first and that physical conditions in which people can live need to be thought of before their aesthetic needs are considered. In any case the colonizers already had the literature of Europe to accompany them. It was to be their sons and their sons' sons who, after their necessary secession from the continent of Europe, would inject a new kind of thought into the stream of literature. This was the thought that in a new land dedicated to opportunity there must surely be created conditions that were more truly democratic than any that could be maintained if the feudal and oligarchal customs of Europe were not discarded. The opportunity for the creation of a new world was not to be missed; it was achieved by a relatively small war—the War of Independence. And there can be no denying that the political literature of the seventeenth and eighteenth centuries was instrumental in achieving the success of the Revolution. This may appear at first self-evident, since all political literature is propaganda of a kind and propaganda is an essential service of revolutionary causes; but the success of propaganda is in strict proportion to its success as literature, and that success was ensured by the quality and appeal of writing such as Franklin's prior to the Revolution and Paine's, Dickinson's and Jefferson's during and after it.

Independence having been achieved, attention could be given to the foundation of a national culture. But still British and European models continued to be influential in literature—and happily so, for as was seen in Chapter Two the colonization of America coincided with the greatest age of English prose. Other forms of art are outside the scope of this book, but it may be noted that in painting, music and sculpture there has so far emerged little that is uniquely American. In architecture there has been the skyscraper, but that largest of contemporary structures was evolved at the dictates of convenience rather than of aesthetic necessity and is only now becoming subject to artistic considerations. As for painting, there was an attempt at the establishment of an American tradition by artists such as Benjamin West and John Copley, who were painting at the turn of the eighteenth century, but it was stopped by the Revolution and too long a time has elapsed for there to be a revival. In music there has been little of interest, only the folk music of the Negroes, which has been amplified into the cult of jazz, and the recent tendency for the Americans to excel in the sphere of spectacular musical comedies, being worth noting.

It was into the stream of literature, then, that the creative spirit of the emergent nation was canalized. The language of Milton and Browne and Burton, of the Authorized Version and Bacon and Foxe proved to be corruptible under the duress of speed and commerce; but no indictment is needed here, for language itself is transitory in its forms and is concerned only with the communication of ideas and the purely linguistic splendours of one age may be merely the scholarly studies of another.

If the characteristics of the American people are examined *via* their literature it will be found that they are, first and foremost, a very self-conscious people. They are aware of religious, moral, political and sentimental problems pressing upon them continuously. They are aware of their cosmopolitan origins, of their paradoxical streaks of intolerance and indulgence. They know all about their own psychology. Metropolitan Americans take a pride in the home-spun characteristics of their regional brothers and the Nebraskan farmer participates in the townee's sophistication through the columns of *The New Yorker*. There is matiness and hospitality everywhere—a heritage from the days when vast distances divided people in time as well as space; and everyone is aware of this *bonhomie* which seems to the Englishman so often so awful. They are conscious too of the mistake they made in importing a race of another colour to serve them as slaves in bondage and of trying to eliminate their guilt in a civil war. They are perhaps conscious of this problem more than any other—unless it is their self-consciousness about their own importance in world affairs. They are conscious of riches and luxury, poverty, degradation and sex; and in these last they are also a little uncertain, and conscious of their uncertainty.

All these facets of the American's self-consciousness may be examined in the literature. One may see the puritanical elements of religion beginning in the diatribes of the Mathers and ending officially with the flourish of a governmental law banning the Klu Klux Klan, but continuing surreptitiously in the inverted puritanism of James Branch Cabell's neo-classical novels. The national ideas of freedom can be traced through Franklin, Paine and the rest, regionalism from Hawthorne down to Faulkner, the awareness of psychiatric states from Poe onward—and so on. And in all this literature there exists, sometimes overtly and sometimes covertly, a slightly belligerent pride in the racial characteristics displayed. Such a pride may perhaps be considered by older nations a little naïve, a little juvenile, and non-literary Europeans may, and often do, smile at the idea of a distinctive American literature. Such people are too often apt to assume that because America and Britain share a language American literature is a branch of English. Such is no longer the case. With the coming of the nineteenth century it ceased to be true and it has not been true since Melville and Whitman imparted the distinctive quality that attracted universal interest to themes that were essentially parochial. When such an interest is aroused uniqueness is attained and thereafter has only to be amplified and expanded by other writers.

This is not to say that expansion and amplification must take place: history will play its part and the level of achievement can hardly be maintained, let alone expanded, without the continuing arrival on the scene of writers of talent. If the question, 'has the achievement of American literature been maintained and amplified?' is asked, the short answer must be No. But a little qualification is needed if the surveyor is to be just.

It would be true to state that *in the circumstances* the achievement has been maintained. But the circumstances have not been propitious for the growth of a literature. The same over-rapid industrial growth that made communication easier and the common man more wealthy—and on the face of things more 'cultured'—resulted in an impoverishment of the aristocratic soil in which literature flourishes best. Whitman, raising the common man to his apogee, paradoxically helped to stultify the growth of literature in America; for the trouble with the common man has ever been that he is common and that when literature or any other form of art concerns itself with him it too becomes common. Literature is best when it concerns itself with peasants and aristocrats. Writing about the common man makes him, and literature, too smug.

And this, it seems, is what has happened in America. There has been a fine achievement—let there be no doubt about that; to produce writers of the stature of Hawthorne, Melville and Whitman in so short a space of time is in itself remarkable. But the over-rapid commercialization of a country rich in natural resources, plus two world wars—war being another great sublimation of the common man—have combined to halt that achievement; so that now, at the turn of the twentieth century, there is a pause. A pause in a journey is not a bad thing: it allows one to take a good look at the roads ahead; and although in art there can be no conscious selection of the direction to be taken when the fork is arrived at there can at least be a consideration of the alternatives.

II

It is best to be bold and state categorically that in the twentieth century there has been only one writer of the stature of Melville and Whitman: William Faulkner. It is not possible in a book of this size fully to indicate that stature, nor to deal with the usual argument put up against the proposition—that Faulkner is too wilfully bewildering in his style; though it may be briefly recalled as a parallel case that Melville was popular only so long as he kept his work at the level of romantic adventure. But as the century turns and the literature of the first thirty years begins to fall into perspective there seems to be little else that will match up in stature or durability to the work of the nineteenth-century giants.

There has of course been an enormous quantity of everything published. Only England seems to have been so prodigal of mediocrity. Looking back over the forgotten books of forgotten months, the Literary Guild selections, the catchpenny 'dividends' and rubbish, it is salutary to note how much of a racket literature has become. The racket is of course only a manifestation of certain commercial principles that are in their turn characteristic of the age of materialism, and the books it produces quickly assume their proper place among the dredgings of literary history. But it might be thought that in the long run the law of averages would ensure that the bigger the quantity of books produced the bigger the percentage of worthwhile books among them. This, however, is not so; for though the law of averages can be applied to the production of books it appears to have nothing whatever to do with the production of writers of quality to write them, who are apt to appear with intervals of two centuries dividing them.

But although American literature may have been halted in its progress by commercialization, wars, and the fear referred to by Faulkner in his Nobel speech, there has been a fairly successful tenure of ground already won: the distinctive quality of American literature, having been wrought from the English language and English letters, has not suddenly vanished in the night of the twentieth century, leaving the territory as English as it was in the seventeenth. It might be said with truth that there has been consolidation and even a widening of the front, but no advancement. Such an advancement can proceed only from a new vitality, an increase in power such as might be forced into the heart by, say, one new writer of the stature of Jeffers, O'Neill or Faulkner. Hemingway has that stature, but has concentrated on writing of the expatriate American—though it must be pointed out that in matters of technique he laid the foundations of a style that has come to be accepted as the quintessence of American literature, just as O. Henry has come to be thought of as a master of the short story.

There are many knowing literary gents—some of whose opinions are of considerable value—who would at this stage point to the work of John Steinbeck, Upton Sinclair, Henry Miller, George Santayana, Pearl Buck (another Nobel prizewinner), Ring Lardner, Edna St Vincent Millay, Frederic Prokosch, Kay Boyle and a dozen others whose names have not even been mentioned so far in this survey. Although such writers admittedly deserve less cavalier treatment they do not seem, in the long view, to have developed American literature except in bulk, or to have discovered any new lines of approach to the interpretation of their national problems. Exceptionally, it may be observed: that Steinbeck, in *The Grapes of Wrath*, drew attention to the problem of poverty among the farm labourers of Oklahoma and that the book was instrumental in securing reforms; that Kay Boyle showed in *Monday Night* a brilliant talent that later dwindled away to glossy-magazine level; that Henry Miller's masterpieces of indecency, *Tropic of Cancer* and *Tropic of Capricorn*, at least managed to get themselves banned in America and England, and that elsewhere his diatribes against civilization assumed fanatical proportions; that Santayana achieved a philosophy combining materialism and scepticism; and that Pearl Buck in *The Good Earth* made a substantial contribution to the understanding of the East by the West. But on the whole they are writers who have helped with the consolidation rather than the advancement or development of their literature.

In later generations there are a number of writers whose work is indicative of promise: Truman Capote, Lionel Trilling, Irwin Shaw, Paul Horgan, Delmore Schwartz, Paul Bowles and Merle Miller have all published work that has been well received but about whom it is too early to speak of achievement. Damon Runyon carved a niche for himself with his inimitably slangy stories of New York, and John O'Hara, using the Hemingway technique, is an accomplished writer of brief sketches reflecting the manners and customs of the metropolis and of two powerful, if despairing, novels, *Appointment in Samarra* and *Butterfield 8*.

During the last twenty years there appears in American fiction a tendency to change its outlook. The general indications are of a swing from Naturalism to Symbolism. The influence here is probably of Franz Kafka, diminishing imitations of whose novels appear too often to be healthy. For both Romanticism and Naturalism are positive in their force and urgency, even though they may both—particularly Naturalism—reflect decadence in their subject-matter; but Symbolism as a literary movement tends to be effete in its method and self-destructive in its achievement.

It would, however, be wrong to imply that Symbolism is a death-knell to literature: the literature of France appears to be in a reasonably healthy state in spite of the works of Baudelaire, Rimbaud and Mallarmé. The prevention of Symbolism's tendency to rot is largely a matter of awareness, and of that characteristic the Americans have never shown themselves deficient. Happily self-conscious even about their introversions, their awareness of their literary plight is best exemplified in their literary criticism—some of which is about the best being written in the language—and in their literary humour.

The literary humour of America at its best is—and has been for the last thirty years—to be seen in the *New Yorker* school of writers. Since they all write to a prescribed pattern there is inevitably a similarity in their styles, their subject-matter and their treatments. Perhaps the best description of *New Yorker* stories is that which James Thurber, one who writes them, applied to his own work: 'The little wheels of their invention are set in motion by the damp hand of melancholy.' *New Yorker* stories are themselves occasionally symbolic; they are more often macabre, cynical, or frighteningly perceptive; they are invariably sensitive, delicately written, subtle and apparently formless (it was once said that *New Yorker* stories were simply ordinary stories with the beginnings and endings chopped off), though the formlessness is usually a subtle Tchekovian shape imposed on them deliberately by the authors. But whatever their shape, size or attitude they never lack the imprint of the finger of melancholy, the touch of pessimism that demonstrates the intellectual American's distaste for the spurious optimism that is being foisted on him by the official 'culture' of the country. This deliberate cheerfulness —which is typical of much of the glossier best-selling literature—is itself part of a façade hiding the aridity that introversively finds refuge in symbolism. And it is entirely admirable that it is critically balanced by the work of Dorothy Parker, James Thurber, S. J. Perelman, E. B. White, Frank Sullivan, Raoul Dahl, Francis Steegmuller and the rest of the New Yorker story-writers. In the work of the same journal's critics and poets one finds (Edmund Wilson and Ogden Nash are brilliant examples) a similar distrust of the look-at-us-how-big-and-rich-we-are attitude that indicates an impoverishment of life as well as literature.

With such an awareness running its lively course through *The New Yorker* and many of the literary reviews that are so admirably produced and edited—most of them with the aid of University funds or grants from cultural foundations—there seems every likelihood that smugness will be corrected and impoverishment held in check until more writers of the stature of Faulkner and Hemingway arrive on the scene to instil a new vitality into the bloodstream of American literature.

A more positive hope for the future of that literature is to be found in the work of Saul Bellow, a Canadian by birth and an American by adoption, who was born in 1915 and has been awarded a Guggenheim Fellowship for his writing. Bellow's first two novels *Dangling Man* and *The Victim* were studies in an introspective anguish that is typical of the personal guilt expressed in so many post-war American novels; but in *The Adventures of Augie March* a very different standpoint is adopted. The saga of Augie March is a vast, sprawling, fast-moving colloquial narrative told in the first person by a Chicago Jew in the period between the wars. In the diversity of its scenes and characters it rivals Don Passos' *U.S.A.*, but there is an additional rumbustious quality about the humour and a picaresqueness in the conception of Augie himself that is far more effective in its result than the intentions of the older novel—and even of such lusty sex-drives as *The Naked and the Dead*. It is a quality that has more than the promise of a shot in the arm.

In the work of James Baldwin, a young New Yorker born in 1924, there is promise of a rather different kind. Bellow is in his picaresque way seeking a reaffirmation of man's faith in himself; Baldwin is seeking not to reaffirm but to establish the individual's faith in God. He is concerned at the same time to demonstrate the number of ways in which the individual can deceive himself through fear.

Baldwin is a Negro but he does not deal with the 'Negro

problem'; in fact he has a good deal to say in various critical essays on the subject of racial equality being ill served by too much protest. In this he is supported by Ann Petry, whose novel on the theme of miscegenation, *The Street*, showed a promise that has not yet been fulfilled, and by Richard Gibson, essayist and short-story writer, whose work is as yet little known in England. Baldwin's first novel, *Go Tell It on the Mountain*, is an extremely compelling narrative telling of the conversion to Christianity of an adolescent boy. The action covers one day only and although everything takes place in a setting wholly unfamiliar to English readers, i.e. a small Harlem Church, there is never the slightest degree of unreality in the description. But even more triumphant in its achievement is the insight into the boy's mind and the minds of his friends and relatives who surround him and help to establish his faith.

Perhaps Bellow and Baldwin in their different ways will prove to be as important to the literary surveyor of the twenty-first century as Frenau, Cooper, Hawthorne, Twain and their successors seem to be today. On the other hand, the works of the slick best-selling novelists with their phoney romantic sagas and their carefully calculated obscenities designed for the release of puritanically repressed emotions, may prove to be the truest revelation of the American mind. However it falls out, the revelation of literature may be accepted as undistorted and unbiased—the true picture of the intellect of a nation.

CHRONOLOGY

Seventeenth Century

Religious writings of the Puritan Divines; early poetry, documentaries:

Smith	Williams	The Mathers	Ward
Anne Bradstreet	Taylor	Wigglesworth	Byrd

Eighteenth Century

Social studies; political writings; literature of the Independence; early fiction:

Franklin	Dickinson	Paine	Jefferson
Hamilton	Frenau	Brockden Brown	

Nineteenth Century

Nature poetry; fiction in the Romantic tradition; satire; journalism; pastoral writings; Civil War literature; the extension of Realism:

Bryant	Cooper	Irving	Longfellow
Emerson	Thoreau	Whittier	Melville
Harriet Beecher Stowe		Whitman	Poe
Hawthorne	Twain	Sarah Orne Jewett	Harte
Crane	London	Norris	

Twentieth Century

The further extension of Realism and the reaction brought about by the demand for escape literature; drama:

Dreiser	Stein	Sherwood Anderson	
Booker T. Washington		Henry James	Edith Wharton
Cabell	Faulkner	Hemingway	O'Neill
Jeffers	Odets	Wilder	Tennessee Williams
Robinson	Frost	Pound	

BIBLIOGRAPHY

General Reference Books

The Oxford Companion to American Literature
The Oxford Book of American Verse
The Penguin Book of American Verse
The Oxford Book of American Prose
A Study of Literature for Readers and Critics. David Daiches

Study Books

The Cambridge History of American Literature
The Literary History of the United States. R. E. Spiller
A History of American Letters. W. F. Taylor
Main Currents in American Thought. V. L. Parrington
The Theory of American Literature. Howard Mumford Jones
The American Novel. Carl Van Doren
A History of American Drama. A. H. Quinn
The Art of Fiction and Other Essays. Henry James
American Renaissance. F. O. Matthiessen
The World of Washington Irving
The Flowering of New England
The Times of Melville and Whitman
New England: Indian Summer
} Van Wyck Brooks
The American Language. H. L. Mencken
On Native Grounds. Alfred Kazin
Writers in Crisis. Maxwell Geismar
A History of American Magazines. F. L. Mott
Contemporary American Authors. F. B. Millett
Literary Opinion in America. M. D. Zabel

INDEX